HISTORIC HOTELS
of the
ROCKY
MOUNTAINS

HISTORIC
HOTELS
of the
ROCKY
MOUNTAINS

Mary Jane Massey Rust

ROBERTS RINEHART PUBLISHERS

Published by Roberts Rinehart Publishers
6309 Monarch Park Place
Niwot, Colorado 80503
Tel 303.530.4400
Fax 303.530.4488

Distributed to the trade in the U.S. and Canada by Publishers Group West

Published in the UK and Ireland by
Roberts Rinehart Publishers
Trinity House, Charleston Road
Dublin 6, Ireland

Cover photo: Brooks Lake Lodge, Dubois, Wyoming; stained-glass transom, Hotel
Boulderado, Boulder, Colorado

International Standard Book Number 1-57098-176-0

Library of Congress Catalog Card Number 97-67693

Manufactured in the United States of America
10 9 8 7 6 5 4 3 2 1

To Carl, Paul, Chris,
Michael, Marianne,
Joe, and Marty—my
children and best friends

CONTENTS

PREFACE

The hotels of the Rockies are among the sole surviving original structures of an era we can access from the records, journals, books, and newspapers of days gone by. Flimsy tents and wooden shacks of old mining towns were utterly subject to the furies of floods, wind, and fires. But the more substantial, often brick or stone hotel buildings, tended to survive and could be restored, albeit at great expense. This is why it is possible today to be a guest in a hotel that once welcomed such frontier characters as Buffalo Bill Cody, Poker Alice, Wild Bill Hickok, or Calamity Jane.

The buildings themselves are repositories of past energies, years upon years of human dramas played out in them. It takes only a little imagination to feel those old presences. Travelers and vacationers who pass up the Holiday Inns, the Motel 6s, 7s, and 8s, and head for a historic property are rewarded with more than just a night's stay.

Some of these historic properties exude a palpable excitement. The bullet holes in the tin ceiling of The Irma in Cody are graphic reminders of earlier, wilder times. Sometimes there is a calm, almost contemplative atmosphere in a venerable, treasured building, such as Denver's Brown Palace. A "down home" feeling permeates the Sacajawea in Three Forks, Montana, with its rocker-lined front porch. Each has its own distinctive ambiance, and part of the attraction for visitors is discovering it for themselves.

The stories of historic hotels can't be told without an understanding of the tangled aspects of western history—the role and eventual displacement of American Indian tribes, the arrival of nineteenth-century goldseekers, early adventurers, and the development of the national park system. It is important to put the hotels in their historic and geographical settings, with attention to what was happening around them and who were the principal players.

Several in this book are also categorized as bed and breakfasts and are members of the Association of Historic Hotels of the Rocky Mountain West (AHH WEST). Many are also members of the Historic Hotels of

America and are on the National Register of Historic Places. Many of the larger hotels in this book provide buffet or continental breakfasts for their guests, but could hardly be considered bed and breakfasts, a term usually applied to inns or small hotels. All are members of either the Association of Historic Hotels of the Rocky Mountain West, the Historic Hotels of America, or both. In addition, most are on the National Register of Historic Places, a designation requiring rigorous attention to authenticity in every aspect.

A review of the history of the legislation regarding historic preservation reveals that in 1966 the National Historic Preservation Act was initiated by the federal government. It accomplished four things:

1. Created the National Register of Historic Places.

2. Mandated action in each state and established a system of financial assistance;

3. Initiated the appointment of a State Preservation Officer in each state.

4. Created the federal Advisory Council on Historic Preservation to advise Congress and the President on related matters.

Single properties, districts, and archaeological sites are reviewed. Entries for consideration are usually at least 50 years old, although exceptions are made for outstanding significance.

Historic hostelries of the Rocky Mountains required enormous investments of money and energy by a long procession of owners. It takes a special form of dedication to maintain these venerable relics, which is why current owners are enthusiastic conversationalists. Their roles of hosts and guardians of a nation's heritage can only be described as acts of devotion, both to the past and to today's guests on their own journeys of discovery.

There are scores of historic hotels in the Rocky Mountain West, each with its special setting and time in history. And all along the way are the ever-present spectacular vistas of the Rockies, sometimes distant and misty, often sharply defined in stunning ruggedness. The Rockies have been aptly called the "backbone of the North American continent." There was another backbone, too—the people of this unique segment in American, indeed, in world history. Some of them built and visited those early hostelries.

Exploration and settlement of the American West were driven by a wide variety of interests, not the least of which was the spirit of adventure. Like a mountain, it was there, and many needed no more reason than that.

The discovery of precious minerals lured some hapless, and some wildly successful, adventurers to the western territories.

Soon railroads, with their accessible links to the frontier, brought thousands of others to see for themselves the romance of the West as glamorized by early artists and writers. Hordes of travelers made it worthwhile for entrepreneurs to build elegant resort hotels of surprising grandeur, and more modest but comfortable inns as well. Many of these hotels still play their original roles, and remain ideal stopovers for celebrating the charm, folklore, rugged settings, and history that so typify the Rocky Mountain West.

ACKNOWLEDGMENTS

Because every hotel I visited provided me with knowledgeable and enthusiastic staff members as well as local historians, I wish to include them here. I ask forgiveness from any persons who have been inadvertently overlooked.

Gallatin Gateway Inn: Colin Davis, Katherine Wrather, Bill Keshishian, Martha Riley, architect Jonathan Foote

Delaware Hotel: Susan and Scott Brackell

The Sacajawea Inn: Smith Roedel

The Peck House: Sally and Gary St. Clair

La Fonda: Lisa Bertelli and Angelika Josselson

Brooks Lake Lodge: Dick Carlsberg and John Russell

The Franklin Hotel: Bill Walsh and Mark Wolfe

Glacier Park Lodge: Bill Flynn and Ian Tippet

The Strater Hotel: Rod Barker

The Stanley Hotel: Patricia Maher, Harry Graham, Curt Buchholtz, Lynn Swain, Frank Normali

Zapata Ranch: George Kellog, Angela Moses, Ken and Laurie Klemm, Hisayoshi Ota, Berle and Barbara Lewis

The Brown Palace: Jane Andrade, Eddie Harmon, and Corinne Hunt

The Redstone Inn: Debora Strom, Paula Mechau, John Gilmore, Wayne Brown, and sleigh driver Billy Greer

Cleveholm Castle: Ken Johnson, Cyd Lange

La Posada de Albuquerque: Rebecca Plutino

The Pollard: Ken Bate

Izaak Walton: Larry and Lynda Vielleux

The Lodge at Cloudcroft: Lisa Thomassie, Judy Montoya

The Plaza: Katherine and William Slick, George Deertracks Tyler, Judy Finley, and Antonia Apodaca

The Castle Marne: Diane and Jim Peiker

Prince of Wales Hotel: Gordon Casey

Boulderado Hotel: Sidney Anderson and author Sylvia Pettem

St. Francis Hotel: Catherine Culver, Inger Boudouris, Don R. Davies, and Richard Lindsley

Alex Johnson Hotel: Jodie Hertenstein, Cynthia Day, Nancy Engler, Tom Griffith, David Wenk, artist Norman Blue Arm, Sonja and James Holy Eagle, Louise Demersseman, Ruth Zilcowski, James B. Thompson

The Irma Hotel: Doug Greenway, Leslie Rolnicki, Bill Cody, Mr. and Mrs. Bob Edgar

The Taos Inn: Paula Deverensky, Carmen Velarde, writer Dee Strasberg, author R. C. Gordon McCutchan, Neil Posey, Mary Stevenson

The Broadmoor: Sally Mayo, Debbie Ward.

To my dear friends:

Author Jean Messinger, whose collaboration on our book *Faith in High Places* set a standard for excellence, and for her wisdom, talent, and patience during our many adventures

Author Ann Zwinger, who held my hand through the early stages of this book and cheered me all along the way

Sue Traylor, longtime friend and moral support through the years, for her generous gifts and especially for an unforgettable trip around New Mexico in search of interesting stories and hotels

Ron Weekes, videographer and editor for the PBS version of *Historic Hotels,* who encouraged me to write a companion book

Harry Graham of AHH WEST (Association of Historic Hotels of the Rocky Mountain West), whose patience and understanding helped make this book possible.

Thanks to the following organizations:

Jackson Hole Museum and Teton County Historical Society
Adams Museum in Deadwood, South Dakota
Historic Preservation Office, Deadwood, especially Mark Wolfe
Sacramento Mountains Historical Museum, Cloudcroft, New Mexico
The Inn at Loretto, Santa Fe, New Mexico
The Headwaters Heritage Museum, Three Forks, Montana
Montana Historical Society, Helena
Corporation for Public Broadcasting
Association of Historical Hotels of the Rocky Mountain West, especially John
    Feinberg, Director
KTSC TV in Pueblo, Colorado, Greg Sinn, General Manager

Quinn & Rychener & Associates, especially Stacy Quinn Rychener
The Museums of Santa Fe, especially Neil Posey
Trail Town, Cody, Wyoming
The Buffalo Bill Historical Center, Cody

To all the others I met along the way who added color and detail with their reminiscences of historic hotels, their times and locations.

To my sister Kathleen Perkins and my brother Bob Massey for devoting part of a well-earned vacation to helping with final proofreading.

Lastly, to Toni Knapp, my editor and steadfast cheerleader, and to Roberts Rinehart Publishers, who believed in me.

ALBERTA

Prince of Wales Hotel
Waterton, Alberta, Canada

Opposite: The Prince of Wales with its mountain backdrop.

PRINCE OF WALES HOTEL
Waterton, Alberta, Canada

Prohibition was the law of the land in the United States in the 1920s, but just across the border at the north end of Glacier National Park, Alberta used its provincial option to repeal Canadian prohibition. A rumor was bandied about that the Great Northern Railway intended to build one of its Glacier Park hotels just inside Canadian territory to circumvent the American law. Whether the intention was real or not, the Prince of Wales Hotel, built in 1927, attracted a lot of Americans who longed to enjoy legal libations while on vacation.

The site on Upper Waterton Lake was perfect, except for its infamous prevailing winds, with gusts that often reached 90 miles per hour. Ray Djuff, in his book, *The Prince of Wales Hotel*, describes the blow that almost did in the project for good:

> *The wind picked up, the temperature dropped and snow began to fall. All construction was stopped. . . . Lumber from the hotel construction site was picked up by the wind and blown high into the air. . . . The gasoline storage hut and timekeeper's shack were gone. . . . Despite the storm, the hotel was intact. . . . The only fault that could be found was that the wind had knocked the frame . . . about three inches out of plumb. Winches mounted in front of the hotel were used to pull out-of-plumb sections back into alignment.*

A later storm blew the building out of plumb again, but this time it was closer to completion and was left as it was. In addition to the winds and snow accumulation of 14 feet, there was the problem of Great Northern president Louis Hill's continual string of changes in design. Doug Oland, of Oland and Scott Construction, builders of the Prince of Wales Hotel, claimed parts of the structure had been built four times over. Because of the deterioration of roads, the hotel's original large boilers were skidded through deep mud to the site by 24 horses and sleds.

Then there was the hotel's name. The popular Edward, Prince of Wales (later Duke of Windsor after his abdication), seemed a proper inspiration. Although he had been invited, as far as anyone knows he never visited the hotel named for him.

The green-gabled, Swiss-style, seven-storied Prince of Wales has 81 guest rooms and a charming British air throughout. Tea is served every afternoon, and Royal Canadian Mounties can be seen on patrol in the area. Until 1944, the bulbs in the lobby chandelier had to be changed through a trap door in the ceiling by a man in a swing seat. Now the job is accomplished by a system of pulleys that allows the great chandelier to be lowered to the lobby floor. Like other Great Northern hotels, the Prince of Wales contains large Douglas fir and cedar tree trunks. They were put in place by block and tackle and pegged together. No nails were used in the original work.

In 1932, Canada's Waterton Lakes National Park and the United States' Glacier National Park were joined by both governments and designated the Waterton-Glacier International Peace Park, a symbol of friendship between the peoples of two great nations.

In summer, the town of Waterton, on the edge of Upper Waterton Lake just below the hotel, is a delight. Strolling visitors stop for slices of wildberry pie—a mixture of huckleberries, raspberries, blueberries, rhubarb, apples, and blackberries! A local herd of Rocky Mountain bighorn sheep wander through town, stopping traffic, both automobile and pedestrian. That they are long-time inhabitants welcomed by townspeople is obvious. All gardens are enclosed by wire fences lest the majestic animals make short shrift of the colorful plantings. And boats of all sizes ply this deepest lake in the Canadian Rockies, whose glacier-fed water remains frigid even through the summer.

There are ghost stories, too. A letter from a Texas man in 1943 claims his wife saw the ghost of a young woman who stayed at the hotel just after it was built. Supposedly, a young bride jilted at the altar jumped to her death from the third-floor balcony.

It concerns the like of myself and my lovely wife Sarah that you all have nasty happenings. . . . Upon returning from a wonderful dinner my lovely Sarah had the dubious misfortune to observe a travesty of monumental proportions. As she left the third floor stairwell, a truly beautiful yet despaired young woman lept to her death from atop the third floor balcony. Most disconcerting was the similarity of the young girls name to that of my fair Sarah. To this very day my lovely Sarah cannot sleep past the hour of the young girls death. A curse that will most assuredly follow my own Sarah to the end.

The Prince of Wales as seen from town is a storybook sight, high on its own hill, with accompanying higher mountains. Inside the hotel, guests sit in the lobby near its enormous south-facing windows, the view changing constantly. Early morning mists conjure up an eerie fjord-like scene, only to be blown away and replaced by bright high country sunlight. At night, a full moon crossing over the lake creates a living postcard, and watchers are reluctant to leave their vantage points until the pageant is over.

The Prince of Wales is closed in winter.

View of Lower Waterton
Lake from the lobby.

COLORADO

Hotel Boulderado, Boulder
The Broadmoor, Colorado Springs
The Brown Palace, Denver
The Castle Marne, Denver
The Delaware Hotel, Leadville
The Peck House, Empire
Redstone Inn, Redstone
The Stanley Hotel, Estes Park
The Strater Hotel, Durango
The Inn at Zapata Ranch, Mosca

Opposite: The Boulderado today. (Courtesy: Boulderado Hotel)

HOTEL BOULDERADO
Boulder, Colorado

The Hotel Boulderado, like most historic Rocky Mountain hotels, has had its ups and downs through two world wars, the Great Depression, and later years of decline and neglect. But the Boulderado differs in one important respect, and that is in its financial origins.

It was 1905 when, in a rush of excitement and confidence in their city's future, Boulder's Commercial Association (a predecessor of today's Chamber of Commerce) formed fundraising committees and sold stock to the public for the construction of a grand hotel. By 1906, the Boulder Hotel Company had been established by stockholders, and a site was chosen. All city residents were invited to participate in plans drawn up by the Redding & Son architectural company. After two years and almost $132,000, the citizens of Boulder had their imposing brick hotel, the tallest building in the city. The name chosen after many months of controversy was Boulderado, insuring that guests would remember it was in the city of Boulder in the state of Colorado. The name was the brainchild of William Rathvon, president of the Commercial Association.

The architectural design called for a stained-glass ceiling over the mezzanine level. Imported from Italy, the ceiling lasted for 51 years. The original floor tiling in the lobby is still in place, and the graceful, cherrywood, cantilevered, five-flight staircase remains to this day.

When the Boulderado opened on January 1, 1909, room rates were $1.00 to $2.50. Light fixtures ran on either electricity or natural gas, depending on the weather. (Boulder's legendary windy days interfered with delivery of electricity from an out-of-town plant.) Hot water and heat were provided by a large coal furnace. Many of the rooms had private baths and most had telephones. But the Boulderado was, officially at least, dry as a bone. The entire state was prohibition-bound from 1919 to 1933. In 1907, the citizens of Boulder had outlawed saloons, and even after the state and national prohibition laws were repealed the city remained officially dry until 1967. Thus the hotel had no bar until 1969. Guests brought liquor to their rooms, however, and a few recipes used by the food staff obviously called for the use of "spirits."

Boulder's Curran Opera House opened in 1906, bringing performing artists of note to the "Athens of the West," as residents referred to their city. Many outstanding personalities stayed at the Boulderado. Ethel Barrymore, Douglas Fairbanks, Sr., Bat Masterson, and Helen Keller were early guests. So was Enos Mills, the man most influential in the establishment of Rocky Mountain National Park, just 35 miles northwest of Boulder. But perhaps the most colorful visitor was evangelist Billy Sunday who, along with his wife and four children, stayed at the Boulderado for five weeks in 1909. Sunday's hellfire and damnation sermons rang out daily from a huge 4,000-seat, wooden building constructed just for him.

The hotel's dining room with its stained-glass transoms was quite formal, even to its pewter finger bowls. Seventy-five cents bought a meal of several courses in those early days. On a menu from March 1909, listings included roast chicken with sage dressing for 35 cents, lobster salad for 15 cents, and pumpkin pie for a nickel.

Boulder and its grand hotel flourished well into the roaring twenties. Under the able management of Hugh Mark, who eventually owned one half of the company stock, the business became a family affair. Weathering the 1929 Wall Street crash, the Boulderado limped along after Mark's death in 1934.

Teddy Roosevelt's heroic portrait in the restaurant named in his honor. Whether he was ever a registered guest is not clearly documented.

William G. Hutson, owner of the Hutson chain of hotels, bought the Boulderado in 1940 and gave it to his son as a wedding present. This was the first time the hotel was owned privately. But World War II severely affected the tourist industry, and maintenance and renovation had to be put off. Not until after the war was remodeling finally addressed: new electric lighting was installed and apartments were created on the fifth floor.

By the 1950s, outlying motels were becoming popular. In order to compete, the Boulderado underwent extensive rehabilitation, to little avail, however. The crowning blow was a fierce snowstorm that broke a glass in the rooftop skylight. The glass shards fell through to the stained-glass ceiling, damaging two of its panels that fell to the lobby floor. It was 1959, and by four months later, both William Hutson, Sr. and William Hutson Jr. had died.

The hotel entered a downward spiral of deterioration. There was no interest in restoring the stained-glass masterpiece, so it was torn down, discarded, and replaced with gaudy red, white, and blue plexiglass.

Then the final blow—the city determined the once-grand building was a fire hazard. An ultimatum demanded that either the five-story wood stairway be entirely enclosed with fireproof material, or a sprinkler system must be put in place. Otherwise, the old derelict would be razed. In 1963, new owner Ed Howard came to the rescue. He had a vision of restoring the building's past glory, and invested $30,000 in an automatic sprinkler system.

Mezzanine restaurant and bar.

Slowly, the hotel made a comeback through the successive management of several owners. When William Brantmeyer of Boulderado Plaza, Ltd. took over, one of his first projects was to create a new stained-glass ceiling that would restore the original ambiance of the hotel's interior. Marie Garcia was hired to piece together some 1,500 square feet of stained glass that was painstakingly installed in sections by a worker who accessed the job from a third-story window.

When in 1977 the Boulderado was made a city landmark, a new era began. The work of earnest restoration was carried on. Original pieces of furniture were gathered and carefully brought back to their proper Victorian splendor. Reproductions were purchased to complete the lobby and mezzanine decor. By 1982, the hotel was entirely restored and once again resumed its place as the pride of Boulder, just as its creators had planned 76 years before.

Today the Boulderado has a 61-room annex to accommodate the throngs of visitors to the city. Great care was taken to create an atmosphere in the new wing that is nicely compatible with the original hotel, even to another stained-glass ceiling by Marie Garcia.

Boulder's first luxury hotel now has three restaurants and three cocktail lounges, a far cry from its dry days. In its perfect location in the heart of the city, the hotel is adjacent to Boulder's popular Pearl Street Mall. No two suites or rooms are alike, but all reflect the hotel's beginnings that featured comfort and elegance. The Boulderado is a perfect headquarters for those wishing to experience the varied opportunities of the area, from the Shakespeare Festival, great dining establishments, excellent skiing, and outstanding year-round outdoor activities, to shopping and sidewalk cafe-hopping.

Opposite: The Broadmoor's
airy mezzanine lounge
faces the lake.

The world-famous Broadmoor hotel at the foot of Cheyenne Mountain in Colorado Springs sprang from unbelievably humble beginnings. In 1880, William J. Wilcox, afflicted with tuberculosis, arrived in the recently founded city. He was "chasing the cure" as it was called then, in Colorado's pure but thin mountain air. Wilcox established a dairy farm complete with a large stone house, an ice house, and a small lake. He called his holdings The Broadmoor Dairy Farm. Very quickly, Wilcox's lack of knowledge and experience with the dairy business led to nearly complete failure. But a young Prussian count by the name of James Pourtales stepped into the picture. Their partnership began to succeed and the dairy flourished. Not for long, however. When Pourtales left the country to check on his properties in what is now Poland, the dairy was subjected to sabotage. Local farmers added gasoline to the Broadmoor's milk can in an attempt to squelch competition.

Upon his return, Pourtales managed not only to save the business, but also to enlarge its scope. He established the Cheyenne Lake, Land and Improvement Company, enlarged the tiny lake, and began to work out a new dream. "Broadmoor City" would provide a country club, hotel, and a casino for the growing numbers of high-living citizenry. Once again, Pourtales left the country, this time on his honeymoon. In Europe, news reached him that all the water in his new lake had seeped away through the tunnels of an old prairie dog town. Then his newly planted landscaping died in the drought of 1889.

Pourtales was not ready to concede defeat, however. In a burst of enthusiasm, he formed the Broadmoor Land and Investment Company, and built the Cheyenne Mountain Country Club, said to be the second country club in the United States. He rebuilt the lake at great expense by resealing its foundation with sheep dung and clay.

On his next trip to his European home, he found his estate in poor shape and in need of reinvestment. Returning to Colorado Springs in 1891, he opened a lovely, two-story, white-columned casino. The casino was in debt within months of its opening.

Then rather abruptly, Pourtales caught gold fever, and his attention turned to investments in the Cripple Creek mining boom, none of which proved profitable. Pourtales, dogged by bad luck in his New World enterprises, finally returned to his European estates with money from a last investment in an Arizona mine. He died in 1908 at his home in Europe.

Meanwhile, the beautiful casino had burned down while trees around the lake grew taller. The London and New York Investment Company was now in charge of the property. Colorado Springs architect Thomas MacLaren was hired to build a new, less opulent casino. Financial problems, perhaps along with a remnant of the Pourtales bad luck, resulted in the deterioration of the hotel and casino.

Enter Colorado Springs millionaire entrepreneur Spencer Penrose and his wife, Julie. They bought an enormous estate called El Pomar (the apple orchard) for $75,000, and shortly thereafter the Pourtales bad luck ran out and the Penrose good luck reigned. Penrose vowed to build "the finest hotel in the United States" next door to El Pomar on the old Broadmoor

A room in the Penrose Suite on the sixth floor where Julie Penrose lived from 1944 until her death in 1957. Some of the original furniture remains in the suite. (Courtesy: The Broadmoor)

property. He hired the architectural firm of Warren and Wetmore of New York, builders of Grand Central Station and two grand hotels, the Vanderbilt and the Ritz Carlton.

The distinctive, off-center tower of the new Broadmoor Hotel began to take shape. European-style architecture was eschewed in favor of a building that celebrated its distinctive American setting. The roofs of red ceramic tiles reflected the flavor of the Penrose home. Steel and concrete construction reduced any fear of fire. Italian artisans worked designs in plaster and colored cement that gave the building its ornate decorative exterior. Both "Spec," as Penrose was known to his friends, and Julie were totally involved in choosing interior designs and furnishings. Their exquisite taste resulted in a degree of opulence new to the Colorado Springs scene.

Amenities included an indoor swimming pool, Turkish baths, polo fields, tennis courts, a movie theater, and tour buses for showing off the hotel's spectacular setting. The second Broadmoor Casino was moved and transformed into a clubhouse for a splendid new golf course.

The grand opening of the Broadmoor was actually a series of glittering events. It was June of 1918 and the country was soon to enter World War I. Penrose managed to publicize his new hotel and support the war effort at the same time. He sent his new golf pro, Jim Barnes, across the country on a fundraising tour for the Red Cross.

Even the classy Broadmoor felt the effects of the Great Depression as luxurious vacations became not only financially difficult but somehow unpatriotic as well. One bright bit of news was the repeal of prohibition in 1933. But even that development did not keep the great hotel from being closed for the first time over the winter of 1935–1936. It opened again the following June and was never closed again. Until his death in 1939, Spencer Penrose continued to invest his vast personal fortune in the Broadmoor. Such well-known attractions as the Pikes Peak Highway, the Pikes Peak Hill Climb and the Cheyenne Mountain Zoo owe their existence to the wide-ranging Penrose interests.

Although rooms have been continually renovated and modernized, and several additional buildings are now parts of the complex, elegant reminders of the historic heart of the original building still remain. As it was in the old days, the hotel is a mecca for the rich and famous, sports figures, diplomats, artists, writers, and politicians. The Broadmoor is a resort in itself, owned now by the Oklahoma Publishing Company, but still devoted to gracious living in the spirit bestowed upon it by Spencer and Julie Penrose.

The tram tracks ordered by Count Pourtales for his "Broadmoor City" proved useful for the delivery of supplies during the building of Penrose's Broadmoor Hotel 1917–1918. (Courtesy: The Broadmoor)

THE BROADMOOR

*Opposite: The Eisenhower
Suite, where the former
president and his Denver-
born wife, Mamie, stayed.*

The 1890s were exciting days of discovery in Europe. In Germany, Wilhelm Roentgen discovered X rays, and Max Plank's quantum theory began the era of modern physics. Otto Lilienthal flew his first successful glider. Freud was at work on the interpretation of dreams, Dvorak produced his symphony, "From the New World." And in the

new world, specifically on the western frontier, a proper hotel was needed for the heads of state, railroad tycoons, and wealthy investors who flocked to the irresistible opportunities in Colorado.

Denver businessman Henry C. Brown, who owned several acres of real estate in Denver, donated land for the state capitol building. But one strangely shaped location he saved for a great hotel, the Palace. Brown hired Denver architect Frank Edbrooke to design a triangular building to fit the unique piece of land. In 1892, Grover Cleveland was elected president, and the Brown Palace began its role as an oasis of elegance in the rough and tumble days of Colorado's mining heyday.

The Brown, as she is known by all who visit there, has operated without a break since August 1892. Built of Colorado granite, Arizona sandstone, and sea sand for extra smooth joining of stone blocks, The Brown is one of the earliest American hotels built with a central atrium. Blocks of porous terra cotta were used for the walls and floors, providing a virtually fire-proof building. Mexican onyx graces much of its interior. In the atrium lobby, six levels of cast-iron balcony railings rise toward the yellow and brown stained-glass ceiling, a replacement of the original. The iron panels of the railings are all identical, but visitors are often entertained by searching for the two that are upside down. Whether by design or accident, no one knows.

The Brown Palace was built almost as a self-sufficient city within the city. Artesian wells 720 feet deep still provide all of its water. Because constant refurbishing is necessary, the hotel maintains its own upholstery and carpenter shops. Its electricity-producing engine room operated until the 1930s. In the kitchen a huge carousel oven, over 50 years old, still provides all the dining rooms with breads, cookies, cakes, and just about any baked delectable guests could desire, including the tempting fare for English-style afternoon tea.

Opposite: Sitting room with mirrored ceiling in the Beatles Suite, where the Fab Four were guests.

Due to the building's triangular shape, there are interesting twists and turns of hallways, and each of the 230 guest rooms faces onto a street. Along the exterior of the seventh floor are carvings of animals native to the Rocky Mountains, sculpted by artist James White-house in the 1890s.

Although known primarily as a place of enduring grandeur, The Brown has never forgotten its obligations to the kinds of pioneers who helped establish its importance. Beginning in 1945, in cooperation with the National Western Stock Show, champion bulls were welcomed and displayed in the elegant lobby. Cowboy star Monty Montana sometimes rode horseback into the hotel, often roping the manager on his way. Once Montana rode right up the Grand Staircase to attend a meeting on the second floor! The climbers and skiers of the famous U.S.

A champion bull enters the lobby of the Brown Palace. (Courtesy: The Brown Palace)

Army's Tenth Mountain Division stayed at the Brown during World War II and showed off their skills and bravado by rappelling from the balconies into the lobby. As recently as 1982 in a charity auction, ten magnificent Black Angus cattle reigned over the lobby from a red carpet just below the Grand Staircase. Animals are not currently welcome in the hotel, but they certainly have added to its fascinating history.

The tradition of English-style afternoon tea in the atrium brings a mix of generations—often grandmothers with their grandchildren who come dressed for the occasion, especially during the Christmas holidays. All the amenities of Colorado's capital city are within easy reach of The Brown's downtown location, but one would need a compelling reason to leave its elegance and doting service.

THE CASTLE MARNE
Denver, Colorado

One could hardly imagine a more ideal, congenial owner/ management team than the Peiker family of the Castle Marne in Denver's historic Capitol Hill area. The Peikers are passionate about the heritage and care of their 1889 stone mansion, now a fancy ten-room Victorian bed and breakfast. Prominent Denver Architect

William Lang, best known for his penchant for tasteful eclecticism, built the elegant home in 1889 for Denver real estate developer Wilbur S. Raymond, who lived in it for a scant two years. Paper-mill magnate Colonel James H. Platt bought the Raymond House in 1893. After Platt died during a fishing trip in 1895, his widow sold their grand castle home.

The next owner was John T. Mason. Mason was one of the founders and first curator of the Denver Museum of Natural History and a world-renowned collector of moths and butterflies, which he exhibited in the third-floor ballroom of his mansion.

In 1918 Mrs. Edwin Van Cise purchased the great stone building, converted it into an apartment house, and lived there until she died in 1937. It was during those years that the castle-like house became known as "The Marne." It is said that Mrs. Van Cise's son, Philip, had fought in World War I's Battle of the Marne, and memorialized his experience by so naming their home.

Two more owners, from 1938 to 1979, effected some rather basic changes. One used it as a center for his real estate business, and the later one divided the building into three apartments, one on each floor. Then for three years, the grand castle was a processing center for the state penal system—surely an ignominious role for such a structure. (It seems to be a common phenomenon for historic properties to sink low in value, only to rise up again when the right essentials come together.)

Left empty for about six years, the Denver pioneer Peiker family rescued the dilapidated, fading beauty by buying it and turning it into a fairy tale-like B & B. Jim Peiker loves to tell about the building's one-time reputation for being haunted. How could neighborhood children resist it? Here was a foreign-looking house made of stone—as if it had been transported from Transylvania—a vacant sentinel of dark proportions.

Just before the Peikers took over, a Father Dowling television mystery was being filmed across the street. The film company used the empty, vandalized building as a coffee break location. The TV

Lobby with staircase.

crew often heard a variety of strange bumps and thumps from upstairs, and were probably very happy to leave. Shortly after Jim and Diane Peiker bought the building, a policeman stopped by and admitted to having made the sounds to provide "atmosphere" for the film crew. He had been serving as a security guard with easy access to the whole building during the filming.

Within one year of their purchase, the Peikers transformed the old relic into perhaps the most romantic version possible of a Victorian B & B. Tired of his business career that had entailed 20 years of traveling, Jim Peiker threw himself (and his family) into developing a traveler's paradise where personal attention makes a difference.

There are plentiful examples of welcoming symbols both inside and outside the Castle Marne. Carved into the exterior Colorado rhyolite stone are lotus-flower designs, and on the carved, wooden parlor mantel are dolphins (looking more like serpents), all said by Peiker to be symbols of hospitality.

The same Mexican onyx found so plentifully in the Brown Palace also adds interest to the Castle Marne's parlor fireplace. On each side of the parlor fireplace is an ancient Celtic symbol of man's care for the earth. The "Green Man" is a human head with leaves for hair and branches of leaves coming from his mouth. Despite his pagan origins, the Green Man is found on most of the great cathedrals of Europe. Surprisingly, it is not too uncommon for him to grace older buildings and homes in the New World.

Architect Lang's beautiful "peacock" stained-glass window on the staircase landing has survived intact throughout the years. In a sort of premonition, the Peikers attached a protective plexiglass covering outside a couple of years ago. When a fierce hail storm savagely hit that side of the building the next year, they knew they would have lost that special treasure. The entry hall staircase with its sweeping oval opening leads the eye directly to the delicately colored window.

The Castle Marne reigns like a queen in its historic district, one among many mansion homes. If you must wander from it, nearby in the rather recently restored neighborhood are several restaurants representing a variety of ethnic tastes. For those who like city excursions on foot, walking tours of the surrounding Wyman Historic District reveal the richness of Denver's nineteenth-century rise to prominence as a Rocky Mountain capital city of style and grandeur.

If business matters simply can't be completely forgotten, all the necessaries—an office with a fax machine, telephone, and issues of popular business magazines and newspapers—are tucked away downstairs on the lowest level, so that they avoid a rude intrusion on the calm and grandeur of the Castle Marne experience.

"Romantic" is definitely the operational word here. Scrumptious, gourmet breakfasts are served in the formal dining room.

Afternoon teas spread out onto a side patio and, by reservation, lovely, candlelit dinners can be arranged. The food is healthy, fresh, and homemade, and the entire B & B is smoke-free. Guests can choose a room or suite furnished with antiques and period reproduction decor, one with a spa hiding behind a lace curtain! Despite the Victorian ambiance, each room has a modern private bath. It's a way to savor the best of two complementary worlds. Who could ask for more?

THE DELAWARE HOTEL
Leadville, Colorado

Beginning in 1860, California Gulch, Oro City, and finally Leadville marked a progression of abandoned gold placer mines, deserted cabins, and a 12-mile ditch for hydraulic mining until, in 1876, three Irishmen discovered a rich silver deposit. By 1878, over a thousand hopeful people lived in newly organized Leadville, and

30,000 by 1880. Already, hotels and an honest-to-goodness opera house stood on the main street.

H.A.W. Tabor, who built the Tabor Opera House, was the town's first mayor and a fabulously rich man. His wealth came from grubstaking others and finally from his own mines—the most famous of which was The Matchless. Tabor divorced his wife, Augusta, and married a beautiful young divorcee known as Baby Doe. They lived in high style until the silver panic of 1893, and by 1895 Tabor was penniless. He died in 1898 believing his mine would one day make them rich again. His words to Baby Doe, "Hang on to The Matchless," were taken so seriously that she remained in the old mine cabin until March 1935, when she was found frozen to death, alone and deserted. The story has inspired an American opera, The Ballad of Baby Doe, as well as numerous books, articles, and a movie. The Matchless Mine cabin, just a little over a mile east of town, is open to visitors in the summer.

It was hard to distinguish between the "good guys" and the "bad guys" in the Leadville of the 1870s, 1880s and 1890s. Some of the lawmen and mine guards were gunmen with unsavory reputations, past lives of gunfighting, and dubious business liaisons.

Marshall Martin Duggan shot and killed a man over an argument about who·was going to apologize after Duggan's sleigh almost hit a man who stepped off the board sidewalk. Duggan was tried and acquitted but later died of a bullet wound himself. Nobody knows for sure who killed him, only that he was the loser in a argument with the owner of a gambling house.

Daniel Ellis, known as "Broken Nose Scotty," got the news his claim had hit pay dirt while he was in jail. He paid his fine and the fines of those in the jailhouse with him. They all went out together to celebrate, got roaring drunk and were thrown back in jail for the rest of the night. Broken Nose, like so many others, died a pauper.

The famous Guggenheim family—Meyer and his seven sons—made the beginnings of their huge fortune in Leadville silver. In 1882, Oscar Wilde, in his customary velvet and diamonds, gave a lecture on art (!) in wild and woolly Leadville. The notorious conman, Soapy Smith, plied his trade with Leadville miners, fleecing

them with his shell game. He was killed in Alaska in 1898 in a gun battle. Other famous visitors to early Leadville were Buffalo Bill Cody and actresses Sarah Bernhardt and Maude Adams.

The hotel sign.

    Equal to the fascination of the Baby Doe saga is the life of Margaret Tobin Brown, best known as the "Unsinkable Molly Brown." Her name, as everyone knows, refers to her heroic deeds in a lifeboat following the Titanic disaster. She was one of several hundred survivors. Molly and her husband, James Brown, had lived in Leadville where he found gold. The newly wealthy Browns then moved to Denver, where they were not accepted by Denver's elite until after the Titanic tragedy that made Molly a heroine.

    Doc Holliday, he of the gunfight at O.K. Corral and several encounters resulting in the deaths of adversaries, was trained as a dentist but operated as a gambler. He had seen Leadville in its earliest days, but when he returned in 1883, already sick with tuberculosis, he reestablished his role as a gambler and as a target for opportunistic gunfighters longing for fame as the trigger-happy Doc's killer. But he left Leadville unscathed and went to Glenwood Springs, where he died of his illness in 1887.

In the 1880s, three Calloway brothers from Delaware arrived in the roaring boomtown of Leadville and proceeded to build a hotel they named for their home state. The Delaware, a three-story building, was part of a block that featured hot and cold running water, gaslights, and steam heat. The Delaware's architect, George King, designed the hotel's mansard roof and its tower that became an important landmark on Leadville's Harrison Avenue, now part of a 70-square-block National Historic District.

The first floor of the hotel was reserved for retail businesses, including a department store, while some 50 rooms were available on the second and third floors. For many years the Crews Beggs Dry Goods Company occupied the street level until it closed in 1980.

In 1983, after being auctioned off in a delinquent tax sale, the property went into foreclosure. A new owner maintained the first floor as a kind of mini-mall. In 1991, the present owners, Scott and Susan Brackett, were faced with a monumental restoration and renovation project. Their goal was to create a true Victorian hostelry with strict adherence to authenticity. Within two years they had won an award for "an outstanding contribution to historic preservation."

According to the Bracketts, one of the most demanding jobs was to create a lobby for the hotel, using what had served as retail space. Expensive surprises followed. When the old ceiling was removed, it was obvious that major shoring up had to be done. Tearing off a wooden wall at one end of the large room, they discovered two lovely brick arches that needed restoring. Sturdy square columns were swathed in rich damask-patterned wallpaper to match the wall treatment.

Today, the lobby is wonderfully and comfortably furnished with Victorian-era antiques, and lavishly finished with oak paneling. One conversation area is outfitted with restored pieces that were discovered broken, abused, and carelessly thrown into several closets. Guests enjoy concerts, murder mystery weekends, and renaissance festivals—activities that focus on the hotel's capacious lobby.

The Delaware's 36 rooms and suites have private baths, period antiques, and heirloom quilts, the latter hung fashionably on walls. The two-room Calloway's Restaurant was added to the hotel during its renovation. A variety of tables, all antiques, create the perfect ambiance for casual, fine dining.

Leadville never became a bona fide ghost town like, for instance, Cripple Creek, but it has had its economic ups and downs. From gold to silver, and in this century, molybdenum, the town's surrounding areas continue to yield valuable earth deposits that keep the economy healthy, if no longer booming. More recently, serious skiers have discovered Leadville's charm and proximity to some of Colorado's best skiing. So it has become a destination for year-round enjoyment.

This two-mile-high city, where visitors quickly learn to slow their pace, is nestled among the state's mightiest peaks. Mount Massive, Leadville's western wall, is the second highest in Colorado's Rocky Mountains. And not far to the south is the tallest of them all, Mount Elbert. Whether guests come for the unsurpassed mountain vistas or for a touch of elegance in an almost unbelievable historic setting, the Delaware is the place to savor it all.

Opposite:The Peck House in 1880. (Courtesy: The Peck House, Empire, Colorado)

THE PECK HOUSE
Empire, Colorado

In Colorado's oldest hotel, guests can stay in a room furnished with bird's eye maple pieces brought from Chicago by wagon train in 1862.

The Peck House was built in 1860 by wealthy Chicago merchant James Peck who, along with his oldest son, came looking for—

you guessed it—Rocky Mountain gold. As he waited for the rest of his family to arrive, Peck made improvements to the little house, creating what was then a luxurious dwelling. Mrs. Peck and her younger children brought with them furniture, china, silver, books, and fine clothes from their handsome home on Michigan Avenue in Chicago. Although a well-read woman, Mrs. Peck still must have been surprised at the unusually fine frontier home that welcomed her to the servantless housekeeping style of the mining community. Running water was plentiful—mountain spring water was piped down through a series of hollowed-out, aspen tree trunks, buried below freezing level.

The Pecks decided to take in guests—travelers, gold-seekers, and investors from the East. The Peck House was to remain in the family for almost 90 years. Located at the eastern side of Berthoud Pass where the stage coach/wagon road began the steep climb up the pass, it was a perfect stopping-off place. Soon the little hotel was known for its hospitality, comfortable beds and fine food.

In the Louis L'Amour novel *Reilly's Luck,* the author recounts the Peck House story with James Peck as a character. At the beginning of chapter seven, L'Amour writes, "The Peck home, always the center for everything in that part of Colorado, had now become a hotel. . . . "

At the time of the real James Peck's arrival in 1860, Colorado was not even a territory, that event taking place in February 1861. The Empire Valley was already replete with gold strikes and rumors thereof. As the new territorial town grew, the Peck House was the scene of such social events as concerts by the Empire Silver Cornet Band, wagon parties, sleigh rides, and political gatherings. Risking encounters with bears, the townspeople joined in the gathering of wild berries that became the jams, jellies, and tortes concocted by Mrs. Peck. Grace Mary Parsons Peck was soon "Empress" to James Peck, already affectionately called the "Emperor."

Immediately following the end of the Civil War, the United States Army sent troops west to end the Indian wars. Many "deals" were made to force the natives out of their ancestral lands. In 1867, some 1,500 Ute Indians entered Empire City (now Empire) and set up tipis to await the promised presents of food, blankets, and sundry supplies from Governor Evans, who would extract a promise from the Utes that they would live in peace. The Ute "occupation" of Empire City presented new challenges for the people of the town. Indian ponies ravaged grassy areas, and the Utes went around town seeking biscuits and whiskey, peering into windows, and dancing at pow-wows. When they offered to perform a war dance, the townspeople, fearing a resumption of hostilities, convinced the Utes to skip that part of their ceremonies. Finally the Governor arrived and delivered the promised supplies. The Utes and their camp disappeared soon after.

Later in 1867, the Ute Chief Colorow twice threatened to attack Empire City. He arrived the second time with war-painted warriors, terrifying the community. Some of the citizens announced loudly that there were soldiers nearby and talked the chief out of his plan.

The Empire Valley can be seen from the front porch.

The warriors left town and returned to their own camping ground, never to reappear.

The Peck House survived all the vicissitudes of Empire City's boom-and-bust mining days, railroad controversies, and less-than-friendly Indian visitations. Through it all, the little hotel built a reputation for its excellent dining.

James Peck built a huge water wheel on Lion Creek behind the hotel to mill gold ore from two new mines. The mill also delivered power for a sawmill that provided plenty of firewood. Peck, the well-loved "Emperor," died in 1880 from injuries and pneumonia, following a buggy accident on Union Pass. After his father's death, Frank Peck assisted his mother in the old family business. A two-story addition was built, and the building began to look essentially the way it does today.

The Peck House was the first building in the area to acquire electricity, and by 1881 a telephone line was installed. That event was celebrated by sending the sounds of a concert by telephone to a Georgetown audience, four miles west down Union Pass.

At age 90, in February 1909, Grace Mary Parsons Peck died, ending a long era of her special brand of gentility and hospitality. Frank died in 1917 and his son, Howard, took over the Peck House but let it slowly slide into decline. His sister, Mabel, did no better, and finally in 1945 the great Empire landmark was sold out of the family. It now belonged to Joseph Emerson Smith, who later sold it to the granddaughters of Adolf Coors (of brewing fame) and Henry Colbran (a founder of the Colorado Midland Railroad). The women changed the name to Hotel Splendide, but in 1972 the original name was restored.

Today, the Peck House is owned and operated by the St. Clair family. Gary St. Clair has been in the hotel business since he was 12 years old. He now reigns as the chef, whose gourmet creations are widely renowned. Sally St. Clair manages the hotel in the manner of Grace Mary Peck, with an uncommon attention to detail, especially in making guests feel welcome and comfortable.

In summer there is a cheery buzz from scores of hummingbirds darting among the hanging flower baskets on the veranda. Eleven guest rooms on two floors are charmingly furnished in antiques, some dating back to the 1860s—remember the bird's eye maple? The Empire Valley with its mountain backdrop stretches out to the south. From the bar and dining room, visitors can catch glimpses of the valley and the incomparable Colorado blue sky with its daily afternoon gathering of puffy white clouds.

While staying at the Peck House, a side trip to historic, museum-filled Georgetown is a must at any time of the year. In summer there are narrow-gauge train rides over the high trestle of the Georgetown Loop.

This mountain heartland offers a plethora of experiences—skiing, hiking, fishing, gallery-browsing, or four-wheeling in the old gold fields. For those who like to take chances, there is the gambling town of Central City about a half-hour's drive away.

But there are no risks involved in a stay at the Peck House, unless you consider it a risk to want to remain ever longer there.

*Opposite: The restored
Redstone.*

REDSTONE INN
Redstone, Colorado

The Elk Mountain Range had once been the hunting ground of the Ute Indians and other tribes who camped at the numerous hot springs on their way to bear and elk country. In a treaty with the U.S. government in 1863, the Ute people were to retain the Crystal Valley "for as long as the rivers might run and grasses might grow." The clash of cultures was inevitable, however. When the area's rich mineral deposits were discovered in 1881, the treaty was broken and the Utes were run off their land forever.

High in the valley of the Crystal River, Redstone was once the quintessential company town. Although a disappointment to gold-seekers, its coal deposits were a real find for industrialist John C. Osgood, who knew a bonanza when he saw it in 1881. He had only to create a way to get the high-grade coal to the Colorado Fuel and Iron Company, another of the wealthy entrepreneur's enterprises located in Pueblo. By the turn of the century, Osgood's domain in Redstone consisted of his castle-like 42-room manor house called Cleveholm, a narrow-gauge railroad, a large inn, villages for his employees, a lodge, a club house, a school building, some 200 coke ovens, and 4,200 acres of land.

Osgood's company town provided each married employee a cottage with electricity and running water, real luxuries at that time. Bachelor workers were housed in a well-appointed and comfortable lodge. A club house provided showers, lockers, a library, and reading rooms with magazines and newspapers in several languages. Osgood's second wife, Alma, purported to be a Swedish countess, was known as "Lady Bountiful" and, indeed, this beautiful woman took the miners and their families to heart. Her specialty was an annual Christmas party with gifts for all the children of the village.

The short-lived Utopian dream had seen its heyday by 1903, when internal business troubles and union activities began to plague Osgood's patriarchal experiment and coal empire. Eventually, his Redstone domain was closed down, and his marriage to the intriguing Alma ended. After Osgood's death in 1925, his third wife and widow attempted unsuccessfully to turn the properties into a resort. The New York Times had once called Redstone the "Ruby of the Rockies," but it took only a few more years for it to become a ghost town. By 1941 the population was 12!

In 1956 Frank Kistler acquired what remained of the Redstone properties including the lodge, the workers' homes, and the Cleveholm castle. Then in 1989, John F. Gilmore (former owner of the Hotel

Jerome in Aspen) and partner Deborah Strom bought the lodge, now the Historic Redstone Inn. It is from this warmly welcoming, comfortable building that the natural treasures and legendary tales of the valley may be explored and enjoyed.

The Manor House, home of John C. Osgood.

About half of the Redstone's rooms are in the original lodge built of native, handcut stone and heavy wood beams. It is furnished with signed pieces of Gustav Stickley antique furniture, and heavy, cast-iron light fixtures of the Arts and Crafts Movement. Stickley's works were "modern-style" at the turn-of-the-century and American made. They were charmingly appropriate for the old bachelor quarters, and today in the Redstone Inn they reflect the craftsmanship, simple beauty, and sturdiness of the work of this pioneer designer. The foyer, with its imposing fireplace, and the large dining room are perfect settings for more of the Stickley masterpieces. In fact, the inn is proud

The hallway in the luxurious home where the Osgoods once lived.

owner of one of the largest collections of Stickley furniture in the world.

The inn's added bar, where meals as well as drinks are available, has two walls of windows and glass doors, facing grand views of the constantly changing mountain scenery. A year-round spa, pool, and health club have added to the inn's amenities, making the Redstone a popular destination for locals as well as travelers.

And what about Cleveholm Manor, Osgood's palatial home? A half mile or so from the Redstone Inn, the castle is now the most elegant bed and breakfast establishment imaginable. Built in 1900 as a home for Osgood and his wife, Alma, at a cost of $2.5 million, Cleveholm, an English Tudor manor with 16 guest rooms, can also be rented in its entirety. Carrara marble, domed bedrooms, opulent fixtures, and gold-leafed ceilings are all part of this magnificent mansion. In an unusual stroke of fortune, many of the original furnishings remain. Most of the animal trophies were shot by the enigmatic Alma, surely as fetching a huntress as ever graced the American West.

In the town of Redstone, itself a National Historic District, there are less than 100 year-round inhabitants. The main street is Redstone Boulevard, the south end of which is dominated by the much-admired clock tower of the inn with its still-working original Seth Thomas clock. The tower has become a double-bedded "artist's garret" for guests seeking unique accommodations.

Along Redstone Boulevard are many of the old Osgood company houses, now homes of townspeople. An art center features works of area artists. The town's old ice house is now a cafe. A general store, a tiny library, a museum, several cafes, and gift shops complete the village.

The Crystal River Valley.

It's just about impossible to decide which time of year is best for a visit to Redstone. Winter presents outstanding cross-country skiing, affording the possibility of seeing elk, deer, and occasionally even big horn sheep. Horse-drawn sleighrides and dog sledding put visitors in a fairyland atmosphere. In autumn the views of golden, quaking aspen trees are unsurpassed anywhere. Summer and spring offer ideal hiking, biking, four-wheeling, fishing, horseback riding, and perfect opportunities for simply enjoying stunning vistas.

There are other important chapters to the Redstone story. One is the Colorado Yule Marble quarry, once owned by Osgood, and successively by others, but now leased from the Vermont Marble Company. As early as the 1880s, George Yule, a mining engineer, had recognized the quarrying potential. From this source at over 9,000 feet, the largest single block of marble (65 tons) ever quarried was brought down on a trolley specially built in 1931 to be used for the Tomb of the Unknown Soldier (now the Tomb of the Unknowns) in the nation's capital. Over the years, snow avalanches plagued the work at the quarry, and after a disastrous flood in 1941, both quarry and mill closed down. In 1990, operations began again under the old Yule name. The high-quality, pure white marble is now shipped to Japan and Italy, as well as to domestic markets. Weather permitting, a half-hour, four-wheel-drive trip from the Redstone Inn to the quarry, where the heart of a mountain is being cut out in blocks, makes for a fascinating and educational experience.

There is easy access from Redstone to some of Colorado's best-known places of natural grandeur. Within an hour's drive are the Maroon Bells, Aspen, Snowmass, Glenwood Springs, and Glenwood Canyon.

When pressed for how he feels about the responsibility for preserving and restoring an historic property, John Gilmore says, "It's like raising a little kid. The child grows and gives a lot of satisfaction. The area is rural and pristine, a real Shangri-la setting."

Gilmore should know, and so will everyone who visits this newborn "Ruby of the Rockies."

Opposite: The west-facing dining room of the Stanley Hotel.

Mule deer on grounds of **The Prince of Wales** Hotel in Alberta.

Marie Garcia's replacement of the **Hotel Boulderado's** original stained-glass ceiling in downtown Boulder, Colorado.

The lobby at the **Brooks Lake Lodge** in Wyoming opens to a view of mountains and a small lake.

The **Irma's** famous cherrywood bar in Cody, Wyoming.

THE STANLEY HOTEL
Estes Park, Colorado

High on a hilltop facing the spectacular Front Range of the Rocky Mountains is The Stanley Hotel. Its white clapboard Georgian-style buildings are an anomaly in this part of the West. Most area resorts are either rustic—known as "Rocky Mountain Stick"—or the Swiss-inspired chalet style.

It was the British Fourth Earl of Dunraven who first owned the land on which The Stanley now sits like a regal overseer of Estes Park. A spirit of adventure brought Lord Dunraven to the nineteenth-century wilderness of the Colorado Territory, and he purchased a large portion of it for a private hunting preserve. Locals chafed at his hunting parties and their riding to hounds in "pink" coats and English saddles. Legal battles and local resentment eventually ran him out. He returned to England in 1884. He'd had the right idea—that Estes Park was a perfect vacation destination—but it would take later developers to realize it should be enjoyed by everyone, not just British aristocracy.

Opposite: The Stanley's Eastern-style front porch.

One of these visionaries was Freelan O. Stanley who, along with his identical twin brother, Francis E., was born in 1849 in Kingfield, Maine. They worked together on several successful business ventures, including a dry plate photographic process and the development of the Stanley Steamer automobile.

In 1903 at age 54, his health failing, F. O. Stanley and his wife, Flora, came to Colorado on the advice of his doctor. The bracing mountain air, sunny days, and lots of rest did their work well. In a burst of enthusiasm for sharing their discovery with others, the Stanleys selected the site for a great resort hotel and bought the surrounding land that was once the hunting domain of Lord Dunraven.

Roads were built for horse teams to deliver materials 22 miles up rugged canyons to Estes Park, originally a mining town. In 1909, the sprawling yellow and red Stanley Hotel with its classic Greek columns and "churchy" cupolas opened for business. It boasted 103 rooms, Colorado's first electric kitchen, an elegant dining room with unsurpassed mountain views, and a dark-paneled billiard room. In the bright, sunny music room was a Steinway grand piano, hauled up from Lyons by oxcart for the grand opening.

The main hotel was built as a summer resort, but just to the south was the Manor House—a smaller version of the main hotel—with its central heating system for year-round use. The two buildings came to be known as the "Big Stanley" and the "Little Stanley." A third building, the casino—now called Stanley Hall—accommodated dancing, bowling, and a variety of entertaining events.

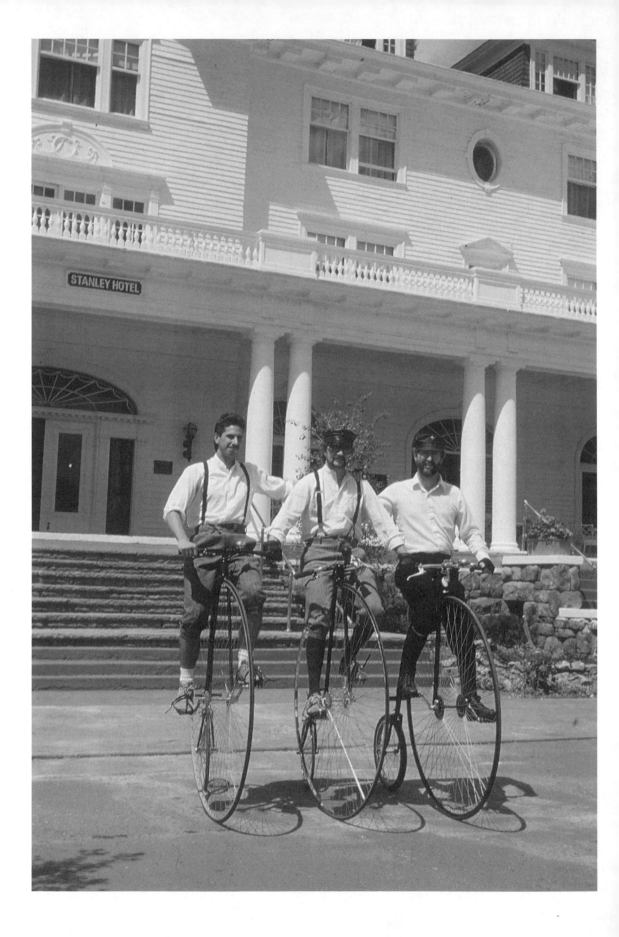

From the hotel, visitors could easily explore the surrounding wilderness. They took horse rides over the Continental Divide, and fished the mountain streams. The highlight of such a vacation was to climb Longs Peak, beautifully framed by The Stanley's front windows.

Early conventioneers were brought up through the Big Thompson Canyon or the St. Vrain Canyon from Loveland or Lyons by sturdy, 12-passenger Stanley Steamers called Trail Wagons. The histories of the hotel and the steam-powered cars are intertwined and honored by the designation of the property as an Historic District, as much for the importance of the steamers as the hotel.

Freelan O. Stanley remains somewhat of an enigma in history. Though he loved high speeds, and demonstrated it often in his steam cars, he had an aversion to driving them in reverse because they went just as fast backward as forward. In town, he parked far from curbside to avoid having to back up, and he had a turntable built in his garage that returned his car to its forward position for departure. Stanley was a dedicated nature-lover who worked tirelessly to reintroduce elk, bighorn sheep and deer to the region after market hunters had threatened their extinction by 1913.

Opposite: 1890s-era high-wheelers at a Stanley celebration.

Along with naturalist Enos Mills, Stanley had enthusiastically supported the establishment of Rocky Mountain National Park. Early on, a wild scheme was hatched to prod Congress into increasing spending limits beyond the provision of basic fire-fighting necessities in the new park. In 1917, in a forward-looking publicity ploy, park superintendent L. Claude Way posed for the Denver Post with a young lady clad only in a leopard skin and dubbed "Eve of Estes." She was to enter the park and stay for a week, proving it was a virtual Garden of Eden. Unexpectedly, a Denver man rushed to declare himself the "new Adam" and headed off to find Eve. Park rangers vowed to protect her, and sure enough, she emerged unscathed a week later.

Resulting publicity brought the necessary attention to the park, and Congress eventually loosened its purse strings. Soon the affair was pretty much forgotten, and the new national park was on its way to becoming the popular playground of natural wonders it is today.

By January of 1982, the hotel had been closed and in a long decline for many years. There were hundreds of broken pipes, and icicles hung on the inner walls. Looters had removed many of the original fixtures and antiques. The unglamorous, behind-the-scenes work of modernizing the electrical, plumbing, and heating systems had to be accomplished before the niceties visible to the public could be added. In May of the same year, the hotel reopened. The painstaking work of refurbishing rooms has continued through successive ownerships.

Winter's beauty can be viewed from the vantage of The Stanley's fan-lighted front windows that look out at the mountain range to the west. Directly across the valley, Longs Peak looms over 14,000 feet high, the northernmost of Colorado's 54 fourteeners. Glaciers carved its distinctive four-sided summit with its celebrated notch. The Stanley is once again the natural stopping place for those wishing to roam Rocky Mountain National Park with its deliciously cool midsummer weather, tundra wildflowers, and autumn's golden aspen.

The focal point of The Stanley's lobby is the grand, inviting, central staircase with its curved balustrades and gleaming white woodwork. Over one of the fireplaces is a print from a Bierstadt painting, a scene that in real life is just a short distance from the hotel. Old photographs in the lobby are reminders that this historic edifice began with elegance and comfort.

The bar and grille is appropriately named for the Fourth Earl of Dunraven. The music-room Steinway, often tuned by none other than John Phillip Sousa whenever he visited, sits regally in its own alcove.

The Stanley, like so many venerable buildings down through history, has its share of ghost stories. Stephen King got his initial inspiration for *The Shining* there, and since then tales have proliferated. One time, the old Steinway was heard, its keys moving up and down with no one in attendance. (It is not a player piano.) The "presence" of a woman in a hoop skirt has been reported by a bellman. In 1994, when Dunraven Grille's pianist played the favorite song of an oldtimer he once knew who had died some time ago, the elderly gentleman's ghost appeared among the guests.

In the spring of 1996, a television crew took over the hotel to shoot a TV series of *The Shining*. Stephen King had been anxious to produce a version of *The Shining* in the setting of The Stanley where he was first inspired to write the book. The renovation necessary amounted to a boon for the hotel in its ongoing improvement and renewal. So King and The Stanley were both winners in the project.

F. O. Stanley died at 91 in 1940 in Newton, Massachusetts, his longtime winter home. He left for the ages the luxurious resort he had created in the rugged beauty of its natural setting. Fittingly, it has often been the site of a gathering of Stanley Steamers and other old-timers that arrive via the old route up through the canyons to celebrate triumphs of other times. The Stanley Hotel is a gracious memorial not only of early grandeur, but also of the need we all have to taste the earth's natural beauty—and one man's effort to allow us to do so in leisurely wonder.

*Opposite: The Strater
today.*

THE STRATER HOTEL
Durango, Colorado

An old story persists that when Spanish explorers came through southwestern Colorado in the 1500s looking for the fabled seven cities of gold, they came upon a river that was to become the subject of a legend. The story goes that after an altercation and a murder in their ranks, the main party of men and priests went on, leaving the miscreants behind. Some time later, weapons and armor were found along the river bank. The Spaniards, assuming their former comrades had died in the river without benefit of clergy to send them into eternity, named the river *El Rio de las Animas Perdidas de Purgatorio*— the River of Lost Souls of Purgatory. A reminder of the old legend is now the area's Purgatory ski resort. A similar story is told of Spanish explorers on the river now known as the Purgatory that flows into the Arkansas in eastern Colorado.

The western-slope river now known simply as the Animas was the site of Animas City, established by farmers in the late 1870s. Their produce supported the miners who toiled high up in the nearby San Juan Mountains.

When General William J. Palmer decided to bypass the little community and establish his own along his Denver & Rio Grande narrow-gauge railway, Animas City faded forever into the shadow of the new town of Durango. A Durango Trust was founded by the railroad company and by 1881 Durango was booming. Helping it along was a smelter moved from Silverton that established a lucrative industry serving the entire region.

Durango fell into the usual pattern for boom towns. Although hotels, restaurants, and shops lined the main street, there was also the usual presence of a tough section of transients, outlaws, gamblers, and saloon-keepers. But Durango, the railroad hub, with its cadre of business people, newspapers, churches, and lawyers, soon became, according to author Duane A. Smith (*Rocky Mountain Boom Town,* University Press of Colorado, 1992), the "Denver of the South." Coal mining, with its proximity to the railroad and the city, insured further prosperity.

In 1887, 20-year-old druggist Henry Strater realized his dream of building the "biggest and best" hotel in the West. With borrowed money, he managed to spend $70,000 for the construction of the four-story, red-brick and sandstone Strater Hotel, which later was joined with the next-door Columbian Hotel. The resulting edifice instantly became the dominant feature of Main Street.

Every room in the Strater had comfortable furnishings, a wood-burning stove, and a washstand. It also had a three story indoor privy with "strategically placed holes." Since the hotel provided a warm winter refuge, townspeople who could afford it closed their homes during the coldest weather and moved into the great Victorian structure. It was the hub of Durango's social life, including a nightly poker game run by a professional gambler. One night, a hotel employee lost his Fifth Avenue brick home in the gambling enterprise.

One of the Durango & Silverton "baby" engines.

The Strater's reputation for hospitality has never faded, but a brand new era began in the 1920s when Earl Barker, Sr. acquired the property. In 1954 his son Earl, Jr. and his wife, Jentra, took over. They soon added an annex and an elevator, enabling the Strater to compete for the tourist business. The Barkers knew the importance of modernizing, so they added bathrooms, closets, and air conditioning to each of the hotel's 93 rooms. They also opened the wild-west-style saloon, the Diamond Belle, said to be named for an early "lady of the evening" who had a diamond stud in one of her teeth. Honky-tonk piano and Gay Nineties-clad cocktail waitresses created a convincing step back in history.

A hotel this large and old is a veritable repository of stories and human dramas. Once, a 16-year-old bellhop was pressed into service to deliver a meal to one of the upper-floor rooms. Arriving at the door, he picked up the tray and checked the number to be sure he was at the right place. He knocked and announced, "Room service." A pretty woman opened the door and stood smiling. The bellhop-turned-waiter promptly dropped the tray—-the woman was stark naked! She helped to pick up the scattered food and utensils, and nonchalantly closed the door. The shaken bellhop was Rod Barker, grandson of Earl, Sr., son of Earl, Jr., and today is the third-generation owner/manager of the Strater Hotel.

Barker loves to share the secrets of the Strater's long history. During prohibition, a bellman stashed illegal liquor under the elevator and established a thriving business selling spirits to hotel guests. Just a few years ago, Barker was summoned to the hotel by an excited employee. It seems a couple of guests had discovered a pistol in a drawer and, thinking it was a theatrical prop, fired it. It turned out to be an 1860 Naval cap-and-ball revolver, and it blew a hole through the bed, the black powder catching the mattress on fire. Although the hotel has tried over the years to locate the rightful owner of the pistol, none has been found. But Barker had a piece of the burned bedspread framed and sent it to the guest couple as a souvenir.

According to Barker, the origin of the word "bellhop" goes back to the days when boys waited in lobbies to assist guests. Communications from the rooms were managed by a complicated mechanical system of wires, hammers, bells, and springs. When a bell sounded, the boys had to jump up, go to the room where the bells were, and see which spring was still quivering—indicating the room needing service. Hence the term bellhop, which today has been elevated to bellman. Barker comments, "When you can look back well over a hundred years, you can visualize the future and contribute to the hotel's existence for the next hundred years."

Most of the Strater's original furniture was made of plain utilitarian enameled steel. Barker's parents, who were bent on stylishness, began collecting antiques. Their first find was in Georgia where they discovered enough Victorian furnishings for four hotel rooms. The process caught on, and over the years, more and more such pieces were found. Rod Barker continued the searches and purchases, and today all the Strater's 93 rooms are furnished with authentic antiques. They comprise the "world's largest collection of American walnut antiques." And there are very few reproductions. To keep an authentic ambiance, such wonders as claw-foot television stands are made in the hotel's carpentry shop.

Chandeliers from Durango's old courthouse hang in the lobby. Part of the front desk is the remnant of a London pub. In the early 1960s, a garage next door was converted into the Diamond Circle Theater, now famous for its old-time melodramas and vaudeville entertainment.

It costs $100,000 each time the exterior of the Strater is painted, a painstaking job that must emphasize its architectural details. Each year, ten rooms are restored, so the hotel's 93 rooms are completely renovated every ten years. The magnificent furniture is carefully preserved, and replacement wallpapers, carpets, and drapes are custom-matched for each room. Thus the elegant side of the hotel's original historical era remains.

When Mesa Verde National Park, the cliff-dwelling home of ancient Anasazi Indians, was opened to visitors, the Strater provided ideal nearby accommodations, and does so today.

An added treat are the steam huffs and puffs of the Denver & Rio Grande's descendant, the Durango & Silverton narrow-gauge railroad. Its "baby" engines pull visitors on a ride through some of the Rockies' most spectacular scenery on the way to Silverton and back. Switching about in their yards, whistles signaling just two blocks from the Strater, they are an audio accompaniment for guests who can close their eyes and believe they have indeed entered a delightful time warp.

THE INN AT ZAPATA RANCH
Mosca, Colorado

Imagine the amazement of U.S. Army Lt. Zebulon Pike who, in January of 1807, came through a notch in the Sangre de Cristo Mountains in southern Colorado and looked down into a valley some 65 miles wide and 100 miles long. Deep snow, broken only by animal trails, covered the valley floor and the sky was an unbelievable blue. On the far side lay another range of mountains, the San Juans, a visible barrier to Pike's westward expedition.

Just before him were huge sand dunes, some over 700 feet high. From the top of one of the dunes, he could see a great river, the Rio Grande, through his glass. He must have been awestruck by the journey that lay ahead. He and his men camped that night in a nearby grove of large cottonwoods. That grove, or "copse" as Pike called it in his journal, is thought to be the site of today's Inn at Zapata Ranch, formerly known as the Great Sand Dunes Inn.

But Pike was not the first to behold the wondrous view of the San Luis Valley. For millennia it had been home and hunting ground to the Southern Ute Indians and other tribes who often contested the Ute presence.

In the late sixteenth century, Spanish explorers and missionaries entered the valley and left their legacy of Spanish names—Sangre de Cristo (Blood of Christ), San Luis (Saint Louis), Monte Vista (mountain view), and Rio Grande (great river), to name just a few. For a time Spanish settlers, and later, mountain men, miners, and ranchers shared the valley—-not always peaceably—-with the Indian bands. Eventually, treachery on the part of the U.S. Government drove the Utes out of their ancestral land, yet to this day the Great Sand Dunes and nearby Mount Blanca are held holy by modern Utes.

Today, on entering the cottonwood grove in spring, one's first impression is an auditory one. It is the sound of perhaps a hundred barn swallows chirping and hovering overhead in the tops of the trees, or swooping to and from their nests in old ranch buildings. This is the parking lot for the Inn where you are also just as liable to see mule deer making their way between parked cars.

In 1912, the old Zapata and Medano cattle ranches were united into one 100,000-acre property and for the next 35 years were under the ownership of G.W. Linger. Subsequent sales and separations occurred through the years, but a short time ago the ranches were once again joined in a purchase by the present owner, Rocky Mountain Bison Inc. (RMBI), and meticulous restoration of the historic property was begun. The Medano remains a working ranch with one departure from its past—-where cattle once grazed, there are now over 2,000 head of bison. The Zapata Ranch is the resort/retreat.

The old Zapata Ranch headquarters now serves as the accommodation area, three different buildings providing guest quarters. Portions of the main building of the old homestead, its rough-hewn logs just as they were in the 1800s, house the dining room and several guest rooms. The original bunkhouse offers more rooms, and a 1960s Texas-style ranch house, built by a former owner, stands alone facing the incomparable, vast sand dune area.

Bison roundups in the fall are managed by "buffaleros" mounted on off-road motorcycles.

All rooms are furnished with a pleasant mixture of southwestern decorations. Many pieces of furniture, designed by the owner of the ranch, were built by hand from old barn boards. A golf shop is located in a renovated old barn and steps away are a pool, spa, and health club, each with its own view of the surrounding ranchlands. The health club offers the very latest in athletic equipment and a wall of glass for taking in the spectacular natural environment.

Driving or hiking around the ranches affords closeup enjoyment of wildflowers, lakes, streams, wildlife, archeological sites, and a variety of historic ruins. It is thought that one mysterious, five-sided, hand-hewn wooden building might have been a Mormon chapel, or a place where religious groups called *penitentes* held their secret meetings and rituals. No one knows for sure. One day in June, though, it was occupied by a mule deer doe and buck, as if they had taken up housekeeping in it.

What looks like desert from main roads is actually a healthy stand of native grasses, the likes of which once supported thundering herds of bison and other range animals.

The presence of plentiful water, runoff from the Sangres, made it possible to build and maintain an 18-hole USGA championship golf course. A series of irrigation ditches delivers the water wherever it is needed. One hole on the course is called "Bison Run" because as the green was being landscaped a few bison decided to plod right over it, leaving considerable havoc behind. Most holes are named for the views they offer. "The Needle," for instance, refers to a sharp peak in Crestone a few miles to the north.

Because bison (erroneously though commonly called buffalo) have been known to gore horses, the ranch manager and his crew of "buffaleros" manage the herd on cross-country motorcycles. Bison pretty much do their own thing, but they must sometimes be moved from one field to another. By rotating fields, the hearty and nutritious native grasses are preserved. In early October, a roundup takes place and some of the animals are shipped out to be used as food for restaurants, including the Inn at Zapata Ranch where bison burgers, kabobs, and steaks are featured. For those who prefer their bison "on the hoof," there is ample opportunity to spot a large herd from the golf course or the many roads that criss-cross the ranch.

There are two special treats for guests involving the bison. In late spring and early summer, a few cows and calves occupy a large pen only a few yards from the Inn. In a smaller pen farther away lives Amelia, the ranch's pet bison. She was only a few hours old and orphaned when rescued. Hand fed by bottle and lovingly tended,

Amelia grew up playful and lighthearted. Unfortunately, her full-grown size and strength now make her playfulness too dangerous for people. So it is a thrill to see this magnificent animal up close.

Using the Inn at Zapata Ranch as headquarters, guests can explore the riches of the 8,000-foot-high valley. Just five minutes away by car is the Great Sand Dunes National Monument, the result of thousands of years of westerly winds blowing across the valley from the San Juan Range. The sand has piled up against the Sangre de Cristo Mountains in a 55-square-mile area. These are the highest dunes in North America and their ever-shifting shapes are a challenge and inspiration to hikers, photographers, and artists.

To the south is San Luis, oldest town in Colorado, founded in 1851. Here, local artist Huberto Maestas has sculpted almost life-sized bronze Stations of the Cross along a trail up the side and on top of a mesa. Local oddities such as an ostrich farm and an alligator ranch are less than an hour away from the Zapata, and natural hot springs are scattered throughout the valley.

Meanwhile back at the ranch, the chef prepares gourmet meals, starting the day with a huge buffet breakfast. Later, your room is ready for the most peaceful night imaginable, complete with quilts and comforters needed for cool nights in the high altitude. Guest rooms have no television sets or telephones to break the spell of this quiet western setting. Before retiring, it's a good idea to go out and face the west for the thrill of a San Luis Valley sunset. The day ends with shimmering gold and rose streaks reflected up to wispy, horizontal clouds just as it surely did for the native Indian tribes, explorers, and settlers of long ago. And as night falls, the calls of coyotes are reminders of other long-time inhabitants of these historic ranches.

MONTANA

Gallatin Gateway Inn, Gallatin Gateway
Glacier Park Lodge, East Glacier
Izaak Walton Inn, Essex
The Pollard, Red Lodge
Sacajawea Inn, Three Forks

THE GALLATIN GATEWAY INN
Gallatin Gateway, Montana

The Chicago, Milwaukee, St. Paul, and Pacific Railroad, known as the Milwaukee Road, built a spur line from Three Forks to a tiny town called Salesville in the valley of the Gallatin River, Montana. It was 1927, and the railroad industry saw a way to capitalize on the great public interest in nearby Yellowstone, the nation's first national park. The Milwaukee Road, sparing no expense, built the elegant, spacious Gallatin Gateway Inn in four months with 500 workers. Salesville became Gallatin Gateway, and a new era of tourism began.

Guests, or "Galligators," arriving by Pullman cars at the inn, freshened up, had a meal or two and then proceeded by park buses to their final destinations in the lodges of Yellowstone. The Inn, like the Milwaukee Road itself, was "electrified" and even had a telephone in every room. Although it was sometimes leased, the inn remained the property of the Milwaukee Road until 1961. By then automobiles and air travel were the preferred modes of vacation transportation. In 1986, with an award for historic restoration under the devoted attention of owners Catherine Wrather and her son Bill Keshishian, and architect Jonathan Foote, the inn had its second grand opening. What had happened between the two openings is hard to believe.

First the bad news. The elegant old building not only fell into disrepair, but it became the site of a variety of damaging and demeaning activities. Old posters reveal that raucous rock & roll concerts and "Ladies Mud-Wrestling" events took place in its large lounge area. The good news is that the structure was never extensively altered. Therefore, its basic integrity survived. Wrather and Keshishian saw the glory that had been buried and abused, and imagined its transformation for a new era. So they bought the inn.

According to Wrather, the overwhelming project of restoring the Gallatin Gateway Inn was undertaken with an almost naive enthusiasm. Bill Keshishian was faced with some nearly overwhelming problems when he took on the physical restoration. Something like 12,000 nails had to be reset by hand for the refinishing of the lounge floor. Workers sat on the floor and scooted backwards as they attacked the protruding nails. Then, a huge

Opposite: The east-facing colonnade was closed in during the building's restoration process.

boiler that was attached to the back of the building had to be removed. It took several tries, but finally the biggest boom truck in the state removed the behemoth from the site. The outline of the old boiler shed can still be seen.

The Gallatin Gateway's charm lies in the anomalies resulting from its railroad origins. Because few guests actually spent the night, there were only 20 rooms in the original building. There are now 35 including the newly added cottage rooms and suites. The ground level still retains the men's and ladies' shower rooms that served those travelers who spent the night in their Pullman cars.

In early photos, the dining room can be seen set up for over 200 people, hungry travelers happy to leave their railroad cars for meals for which the Gallatin Gateway was famous. The room is now more spaciously arranged for guests who come to enjoy the seasonal varieties of cuisine, often referred to as "Montana's Best."

Where once there was a shoeshine stand, the space is now a decorated alcove in the lobby. The original switchboard, although it is not connected for service, adds some historicity behind the reception desk. The lobby's original railroad clock still runs, and the bar is called "The Baggage Room" because that's what it once was. Over the years, guests like actor "Slim" Pickins left messages and impressions on its walls that add to the room's charm. The old wooden telephone booths, technically modernized, still grace the lobby area. The lobby proper, with its checkerboard floor and beamed ceiling, declares its railroad heritage.

An east-facing colonnade closed in during the restoration has been made into an overflow dining area. Almost palatial, the magnificent Spanish Colonial lounge features large, arched windows that draw in the Montana landscape. An enormous fireplace is the center of a conversation area.

The Gallatin Valley's spreading ranches reach out to the nearby Madison Range of the Rockies. Pathfinders John Bozeman and Jim Bridger once led immigrant trains to the area when it was still home to numerous American Indian tribes. In spring, field upon field of wildflowers bloom as if to bestow a new meaning to the state's official name, the "Treasure State." The Flathead Indian name for the valley was "Valley of the Flowers." And it was once known as the "Sweet Pea Capital of the World." Also popularly known as "Big Sky Country," Montana is somehow larger than life and a humbler of mere mortals.

Predictably, the area is a dream come true for outdoor-loving people, especially those who fish or want to learn how. A specially built casting pond allows them to try out the techniques taught in the on-site Orvis-endorsed fly fishing school.

It would be impossible to overlook Yellowstone National Park in any story of the area. The Gallatin Gateway is 80 miles from the west entrance, and all along the way are the national forests, mountain ranges, and river valleys of Montana's high country. The great park with its natural wonders, scenic grandeur, and free-roaming wildlife will always pull people to the region.

The Gallatin Gateway Inn, built originally as a stopover on the way to Yellowstone, is more than that today. As a year-round destination, it now attracts skiers, nature lovers, and the ever-increasing numbers of travelers who are rediscovering the American West. Visitors may arrive looking for a piece of western railroad history or a retreat in the vast Montana highlands. What they find is a casual, but nonetheless elegant historic hotel to enjoy and return to time after time.

GLACIER PARK LODGE
East Glacier, Montana

By 1891, the Great Northern Railway stretched across the new state of Montana through Marias Pass, just south of a wilderness area of uncommon beauty that was to become Glacier National Park. When the area was established as a national park in 1910, Great Northern's president, Louis Hill, began a symbiotic relationship between his railroad and the wilderness area through which snaked the Continental Divide of the Rocky Mountains. Hill's advertising campaign to "See America First" brought thousands to the West at a time when increasing unrest leading to World War I diminished enthusiasm for European travel. Hill understood well that affluent travelers would require comfortable and attractive lodgings. So between 1913 and 1927, he built four great hotels and several chalets in and near Glacier National Park. They were operated by the Great Northern until 1961.

In 1916, author Mary Roberts Rinehart wrote an account of her trip by train to Glacier Park:

West. Still west. An occasional cowboy silhouetted against the sky, thin range cattle; impassive Indians watching the train go by . . . Then at last, at twilight, Glacier Park Station . . . and an old Chief Three Bears, of the Blackfeet wonderfully dressed and preserved at 93. . . . It was rather a picturesque party. I confess that no excursion . . . gave me a greater thrill than the one that accompanied that start the next morning from the Glacier Park Hotel to cross the Continental Divide.

The Glacier Park Hotel mentioned by Rinehart, now known as Glacier Park Lodge, lies at the east entrance to the park. The site was purchased from the Blackfeet Nation whose reservation just across the railroad tracks still adjoins the lodge property. The main building and its attached annex were completed by 1914, and still serve as the business hub of the park's hotel system.

As if conceived in competition with its spectacular natural setting, the lodge's lobby is almost a heart-stopping sight. Thirty 40-foot Douglas firs, their bark still intact, stretch up towards the 52-foot ceiling where skylights allow sunlight to flood the room below. The trees, natives of the West Coast, were shipped by flatbed railcars. They are said to be from 500 to 800 years old. Blackfeet, watching the building take shape in 1913, dubbed it "Big Tree Lodge."

Main-floor rooms in the annex have individual verandahs, perfect for afternoon margaritas or just admiring the giant firs and

cedars used in the interior and exterior construction of the monumental hotel. Sixty-one of the guest rooms in the main building surround the great lobby on three levels, beginning on the second floor, all of which afford a bird's eye view of the massive columniated heart of the building. There are now 154 rooms in all,

Lake McDonald Lodge's lobby has a charm all its own.

a cocktail lounge, dining room, swimming pool, and nine-hole golf course.

Old hotels, like old theaters or, for that matter, old homes, tend to house ghosts. Hotel managements are divided on how to handle the sometimes very persistent stories. Some boast of them, admitting that the stories add to the charm of their hostelries. Others would rather not mention them at all, for fear that guests would be intimidated.

Of course, a "friendly" ghost is more often tolerated than the threatening variety. In 1987, Glacier Park Lodge received a letter saying, in part, the following:

> *Just prior to dawn something started to "ruffle" the sheets over by my wife and this woke her up. At this time, something sat on the edge of the bed. She felt the bed go down and she was "frozen". When that something moved from the edge of the bed, she was able to touch me and wake me up. Her body was ice cold.*
>
> *I turned on the light and over by the fireplace, the rocker was rocking.*
>
> *We then got up, did not shower, but packed and left!!!*
> *We wanted to get the hell out of that room.*

There are "ghostbuster" types who enjoy every minute just waiting for such experiences. They seek out the specific legendary rooms and hope not to be disappointed.

Although most visitors now arrive by car, it is still possible to relive earlier adventures by taking the Amtrak train that stops at East Glacier station just across the highway from the lodge. Flower-lined walks lead to the front entrance.

Pack trips on horseback were once favorite excursions of the more adventuresome visitors. They wound their way across the park, using its sturdy, stone chalets as stopovers. Other guests lounged away their vacations in the rustic elegance of the park's hotels. It is possible now to drive the park roads, although there are length and width limits for vehicles. Narrow and twisting, the paved roads are not attempted by timid or inexperienced drivers.

By far the best way to see the park, with its 50 active glaciers, jewel-like lakes, northern wildlife, and majestic mountains, is to ride a "jammer" bus. The 32 famous, bright-red jammers were manufactured in the 1930s by the White Motor Company. They take up to 18 passengers, and their roll-back canvas tops allow panoramic viewing. The name harks back to the old days of standard transmissions.

Drivers could be heard from far off "jammin" the gears as they tackled the mountain roads. Now equipped with automatic transmissions, the jammers make easy work of crossing the Continental Divide on Going-to-the-Sun Highway, whose name conveys the park's wonder best of all.

All Glacier Park hotels, including Alberta's Prince of Wales, are operated by Glacier Park, Inc. They are closed from late September to May.

Opposite: Izaak Walton Inn, named for the seventeenth-century English fly fisherman who wrote The Compleat Angler *(still in print).*

IZAAK WALTON INN
Essex, Montana

Eighteen miles from the Continental Divide, the Amtrak train stops twice a day at Essex, Montana, the site of the Izaak Walton Hotel. Outside of the hotel, there is little else in the way of a downtown. But extensive railroad tracks, sidings, and waiting "helper" engines give away the area's role in history. Essex began around 1890 as a jumping-off place for men who, on foot, kept winter and spring snow off the tracks of the Great Northern Railway. Others who tended the helper engines were stationed there.

The railroad company had contracts with local lunch counters to cater to the crews who stayed without their families in the remote little town. Eventually, arrangements were made with private homeowners. The first "beanery," or private cafe, was built in 1909 on the site of today's hotel. It and various other short-lived lunch counters and boarding houses succumbed to a series of devastating fires, the last one in 1935. For four years, the railroad workers were pretty much on their own in finding places to live and eat. Some were meagerly accommodated in railroad "outfit" box cars. Conditions resulted in a loss of employees willing to work there, especially those in snow service.

Finally, in 1939, when the town was temporarily known as Walton, a proper hotel—the Izaak Walton—was built by the Addison Miller Company, a subsidiary of the Great Northern. Izaak Walton was a seventeenth-century English fly-fishing enthusiast and writer. His book *The Compleat Angler,* still in print, extols not only sport fishing, but also a life close to nature. The hotel housed 29 bedrooms, 10 bathrooms, and a general store. Its site was chosen in the hope that an entrance to Glacier National Park would be located in the vicinity, but that never happened. So the hotel was quite overbuilt, and for years, under a variety of owners and managers, it hardly showed a profit. Glacier National Park is immediately adjacent to Essex, but the official east and west park entrances are a few miles away. In their delightful and informative book, *Izaak Walton Inn,* Gail and Jim Atkinson refer to the hotel as the "Inn Between."

Today's owners, Larry and Lynda Vielleux, have lovingly upgraded the historic building. The hotel is warm and comfortable, and each room and suite now has a private bath. Handmade quilts and rustic furnishings add to its charm. The provision of skis, sack lunches, and mountain bikes lure visitors to explore the mountains on their own, but tours on the famous "Jammer" buses are also available. After strenuous daytime activities, guests can mellow out in the sauna or relax in front of the big stone fireplace in the lobby. In winter, skiers

who just can't get enough in daylight hours can ski at night on Starlight Trail, lighted until 11 p.m. Average annual snowfall is well over 20 feet.

Guests may choose to stay in their own private caboose.

The dining room affords unobstructed views of freight train traffic and the nearby mountains. At the far end of the room is a stained-glass seal of the Great Northern Railroad, a reminder of the hotel's origins.

One absolutely delightful and unique surprise is the presence of four retired, brightly-painted cabooses—each mounted on its own piece of track—that overlook the hotel from a hilltop just across the train tracks. The cozy cabooses, with their beautiful horizontal pine-board interiors, serve as self-contained cabins with stove, refrigerator, microwave, and souvenirs of railroad heritage. In the Blue Caboose, bedspreads and curtains are fashioned of traditional blue and white striped engineer-cap fabric. These imaginative lodgings are perfect

Inside each caboose is a cozy bedroom, shower, loft, and kitchen.

starting points for far-ranging cross-country ski and hiking trails. And always, there is the sound of trains whistling their coded messages as they arrive and depart.

Even non-railroad buffs become enthralled with the ubiquitous reminders of the town's involvement in Iron Horse history with accounts of derailments, avalanches, and broken wheels that contributed to the list of catastrophes. Wrecking trains and crews, often accompanied by doctors, were sent to accident sites. Steam-powered, self-propelled rotary snow plows plied the tracks wherever needed. One avalanche is said to have hurled six cars 200 feet down a mountainside. Trackwalkers once covered the entire line daily throughout the year, starting at each end and meeting in the middle. They looked for any kind of trouble—fires, mud, snow, and rock slides. In the hotel's bar is a wonderful collection of railroading photos, many of famous wrecks.

During the early twentieth-century westward expansion, "immigrant" trains brought settlers to Montana, including Essex. Specially adapted boxcars were rented by several families together, whose animals and household goods came along on the same train. It wasn't until 1930 that an automobile road was built, enabling travelers to arrive in Essex by car over Marias Pass on the Continental Divide.

In the yards, just steps away from the Izaak Walton, helper engines await their assignments as they did a hundred years ago. Even today's modern diesel freight trains need them for the laborious trips over Marias Pass. Along the mountainside rights-of-way, wooden sheds stretch protectively over locations where avalanches remain a threat. When there is a derailment, all sorts of government entities become involved. The EPA must inspect the spilled contents, and the Department of Fish and Game requires quick cleanups to prevent wildlife feeding areas from becoming polluted—all this in addition to uncounted business and insurance settlements. In wilderness regions, railroading can be appallingly expensive.

Visitors to the Izaak Walton are given printed safety tips that also contain information about possible encounters with bears, both black and grizzly:

1. Avoid surprising bears. Alert bears to your presence by making noise. The human voice carries better than "bear bells."

2. Solo hiking is not recommended.

3. Do not approach bears for any reason.

4. All bears, regardless of how cuddly they look, are potentially dangerous.

Is all this off-putting? No, it's a way of making visitors aware they are in wild bear habitat. And besides, confrontations with bears are very rare. Visitors always hope for a glimpse of these great omnivores—from a safe distance, of course.

Larry, Lynda, and all the staff clearly enjoy both the million-acre wilderness they live in, and the skiers, hikers, and railroad enthusiasts who vacation at the Izaak Walton.

*Opposite: The Pollard
Hotel.*

THE POLLARD HOTEL
Red Lodge, Montana

Red Lodge, Montana, was a different kind of Rocky Mountain mining community. European settlers, beginning with the Finns, came not to prospect for gold but to ranch and, eventually, to mine coal. French trappers worked the area in the 1700s, and there is evidence of Spanish explorers even earlier. But long before, American

Indians roamed and lived in the game-rich area. Legend has it that a Crow band inhabiting the banks of Rock Creek erected elk and buffalo tipis, painting them with red clay from the surrounding mountains. In 1882, a part of the Crow Reservation was opened for ranching and mining homesteaders, and the town that formed at Rock Creek took the name of Red Lodge. The first pioneers traveled four days to Billings for supplies, although herds of deer provided them with ample meat.

In 1887, the Rocky Fork Coal Company began operations in the Rock Creek River Valley. One year later there was a town of shacks, a logging camp, tent houses, and a "hotel" that was part tent and part log. The marshal was "Liver Eating" Johnston, who steadfastly denied he ever ate the livers of Indians he had killed. The name stuck, however, and his grave in Cody, Wyoming, is so marked.

By the time the Northern Pacific Railway arrived in 1889, there were over 1,000 people in town, including the Chinese who were brought in to finish the branch railway. Saloons were more plentiful than shops. Such famous characters as Buffalo Bill Cody and Calamity Jane came to visit and gamble. Traffic was often snarled by some 200 range cattle that roamed the streets. Curious Indians wandered in to investigate the white man's settlement. Red Lodge was finally properly platted, having grown up haphazardly around the railroad buildings. In the early 1890s the community had a brief bout of gold fever, but the shallow placer digs very quickly gave out and so did the disappointed prospectors.

A carriage met passengers at the railroad station and took them to the coal company's hotel that opened as the Spofford on July 4, 1893. It was the first brick building in Red Lodge. The name was changed shortly thereafter to The Pollard, after the new owner.

Opposite: The town's namesake greets visitors as they enter Red Lodge.

The town's first coal mining disaster occurred in 1906 when eight men were killed. Other accidents and the Great Depression closed many mines, but the final tragedy was an explosion in the Smith mine in 1943. Miners from surrounding towns, and even as far away as Salt Lake City, hurried to the site to assist in

The grandeur of the surrounding Montana landscape.

rescue operations. There were no survivors. It took eight days to bring the 74 bodies to the surface. It was Montana's worst mining accident. By 1958, after more accidents, all area mines were abandoned.

In the old days, according to the updated journal of Barbara Pollard Sanford, the Pollard Hotel housed 60 rooms, a large retail store, billiard tables, bowling alley, barbershop, and basement sample rooms for traveling salesmen. So "uptown" was the new hotel that broiled lobsters were a specialty of the dining room, and a free midnight lunch was served. The hotel's telephone number was 1, and it still is.

According to *The History of Red Lodge* by Shirley Zupan, Buffalo Bill Cody once brought a large party of dudes from the East by train for an overnight stay at the Pollard. Cody arranged with the stable man to add two unbroken horses to the coach team. Next morning, the coach careened up to the hotel and Cody pushed his guests aboard. He then took the reins himself for the trip to the town he founded, Cody, Wyoming. The coach left town "in a cloud of dust." It was a ride none would forget, although Cody confided to his guests that he was a bit disappointed that the horses were so tame.

In the early 1920s, Robert Schendel bought the hotel from the Pollards. He seems to have done only two things: he added wash basins to the rooms and changed the numbering of the rooms, leaving confusion behind for the family when they brought back the hotel.

Thomas F. Pollard died in 1942. Mrs. Pollard stayed on until 1946 when she sold the hotel to Mrs. Lottie Salki, who changed its name to The Chief Hotel. In the 1970s it was given yet another name, Cielo Grande, by Fred Mackaman, the new owner. The Cielo Grande Corporation's extensive renovation plans resulted in the historic landmark ending up on the auction block. It stood closed and boarded up until 1991.

Today's owner, David Knight, represents a long succession of owners and managers devoted to the preservation of Red Lodge's and the Pollard's history.

The Pollard Hotel was extensively renovated in 1993. In fact, its interior was almost completely gutted and then rebuilt in authentic turn-of-the-century style. The impression is one of an old building somehow miraculously made new. The locally fired brick exterior has survived beautifully. It took two years to complete the historic restoration. Outside perimeter rooms are furnished to keep the period flavor and offer sweeping views of the historic town and nearby mountains. A gallery atrium in the center of the building is surrounded by the private balconies of beautifully furnished suites with hot tubs. There are 36 guest rooms and suites, a health club, and a lovely reading room called the History Room. Every inch of the hotel is smoke free. The dining room features relaxed, unhurried gourmet meals.

Most of Red Lodge's commercial district is on the National Register of Historic Places. Hollywood comes to town often to take advantage of the Beartooth Mountain scenery and the open wilderness vistas. The Beartooth Highway, closed in winter, is one of the nation's 52 National Scenic Byways. It provides a spectacular trip from Red Lodge to Yellowstone National Park, reaching elevations of well over 10,000 feet.

There are 25 miles of trails at Red Lodge Mountain Ski Area, and the town hosts the national finals of ski-joring each year. Ski-joring (pronounced "yoring") involves pulling a skier behind a horse. Perhaps the most far-fetched area summer activity is pig racing, which raises money for scholarships for local students.

It took years, but Red Lodge has successfully made the switch from a mining economy to a tourist, nature, and sports-related one. Deer, elk, and other wildlife abound. Moose often roam through the town in winter when the cold drives them to lower elevations. So it is perfectly logical and appropriate that the town's historic hotel has chosen the moose for its trademark.

Opposite: Sacajawea Inn
as it looks today.

THE POLLARD HOTEL

SACAJAWEA INN
Three Forks, Montana

The story of the Sacajawea Inn and how it got its name reaches back some 200 years in western U.S. history. In 1803, President Thomas Jefferson signed a treaty with the French to purchase all the land drained by the Missouri River and its tributaries. The Louisiana Purchase opened up a chance to extend the "external commerce of the

United States." In May of 1804, the Corps of Discovery, or as it is better known, the Lewis and Clark Expedition, set out up the Missouri River under orders from the president. By November, Captains Meriwether Lewis and William Clark prepared to stop for the winter near what is now Bismark, North Dakota. It was there they met the Shoshone girl, Sacajawea.

Sacajawea and her two-month-old son joined the expedition preparing to leave the winter camp to continue up the Missouri. For a year and a half, the Indian girl was an important companion of the men of the exploration party. She was not, as is popularly believed, a true guide—the river pretty much sufficed—but her ability to speak the Shoshone language was of real importance. She knew where to find edible, nutritious roots and plants that could be gathered to supplement every meal's mainstay—meat from wild animals. She also saved a pack of important equipment that tumbled out of a boat during a squall, and she could identify the presence of differing tribes by the prints from their moccasins. And through it all, Sacajawea carried her baby son.

On July 22, 1805, Sacajawea recognized the country they had reached as a place where three rivers met. The two leaders named them Gallatin (for the Secretary of the Treasury), Jefferson, and Madison (then Secretary of State). They are the forks of Three Forks, and the headwaters of the Missouri River.

Quasi-historical and fictional accounts of Sacajawea's role in the Lewis and Clark Expedition and indeed, her life afterward, have idealized the young Shoshone woman as a courageous guide of great beauty. Authors Ella E. Clark and Margot Edmonds used "Original Journals of the Lewis and Clark Expedition, 1804–1806" and other early sources to seek out the authentic Sacajawea. Their book, *Sacajawea of the Lewis and Clark Expedition* (University of California Press, 1979), claims that whatever her historical role might have been, she was "no less of a national heroine for having been at the same time a human being." The most

Opposite: An artist's conception of Sacajawea at the Buffalo Bill Historical Center in Cody, Wyoming.

lasting version of her life claims she died in 1885 at around 100 years of age. Indeed, a grave so marked is on the Wind River Reservation in Wyoming.

Where the three rivers met was a crossroads for a diversity of high plains American Indian tribes, and fierce battles among them were fought in the vicinity. It was a land rich in wildlife, which is what attracted white trappers and traders. In April of 1810, members of the new Missouri Fur Company arrived at the confluence and quickly built a fort, knowing that the Blackfeet were somewhat less than friendly. In fact, the Indians were determined to drive the white men out. The combination of hostile natives and huge marauding grizzlies accomplished that objective before a year was up. It was to be post Civil War before there was serious consideration of a permanent settlement in the area. In 1867, some traces of the old fort could still be seen. An anvil from the site is a treasured exhibit at the Headwaters Heritage Museum in Three Forks, about two blocks from the Sacajawea Inn.

The oldest part of Three Forks was the site of a toll station for the growing number of bridges in the region. Stage coaches and oxen trains plied their way across the cottonwood bridges, their drivers often paying tolls in gold dust. In 1882, the town was officially named Three Forks. By 1883, there were 23 bridges of varying sizes, and business was brisk, both at the toll houses and the hotel.

The town's hotel, built in 1882, was uncommonly large for its time. It could accommodate up to 100 guests, and often served 240 meals in a day. A favorite local story involves the moving of the old hotel in 1910 to its present higher ground location, on orders of the new owner, railroad magnate John Quincy Adams. It seems that after a day of hard work getting the building on log rollers and hitching up his team of horses, darkness had settled in, and the man hired to do the moving decided to take a break in a nearby saloon. He joined a poker game and, in an extraordinary losing streak, managed to bet away his horses. But the animals that now belonged to someone else still accomplished the move.

Owner Adams added what is now the main building, and the enlarged hotel soon began serving passengers headed for Yellowstone Park via the Milwaukee Railroad.

Current owner Smith Roedel tells an amusing story about the mounted deer head in the lobby. When Roedel bought the hotel a few years ago, the former owner insisted upon taking the trophy with her. Patrons soon complained about the loss, so Roedel went to a local taxidermist who explained that there was no similar head available, but he could fashion a composite. That one now hangs where the old one did, and only two people (both hunters) have noticed that the head is from a muledeer and the antlers from a white tail.

There are 33 turn-of-the-century rooms with bath in the historic Sacajawea Inn. An honest-to-goodness, wraparound porch, complete with a long row of rocking chairs, evokes a nostalgia for other, simpler times. High ceilings, original light fixtures, and antique-inspired furnishings and decor create a feeling of "going to Grandma's." Contemporary niceties assure that modern comforts are not sacrificed, however.

The confluence of the three rivers is a good place to contemplate the importance of the mighty one they combine to form, and to try to imagine the life of the teenage Shoshone girl and her baby who accompanied the explorers. The porch of the Sacajawea is for rocking and taking time to try to put it all in perspective.

NEW MEXICO

Hotel St. Francis, Santa Fe
La Fonda, Santa Fe
La Posada de Albuquerque, Albuquerque
The Lodge at Cloudcroft, Cloudcroft
The Plaza Hotel, Las Vegas
The Historic Taos Inn, Taos

Opposite: Front entrance of the St. Francis, just a block from Santa Fe's central plaza.

HOTEL ST. FRANCIS
Santa Fe, New Mexico

La Villa Real de la Santa Fe de San Francisco de Asis—The Royal City of the Holy Faith of Saint Francis of Assisi—is the oldest capital city in the United States. Now known simply as Santa Fe, the city lies 7,000 feet above sea level, surrounded by the pueblos of descendants of the Anasazi, or Ancient Ones—early inhabitants of New Mexico.

The influence of that culture is immediately apparent in the Pueblo-style architecture of Santa Fe, which, by 1957, was officially established by the city as required architecture for its historic sections. Thus, arriving there, one enters a unique environment of unparalleled charm.

Eighty years before the Pilgrims landed at Plymouth Rock, Spanish conquistadors brought an alien culture to the people who lived in and around what is now Santa Fe. The strangers were looking for gold. By 1609, however, the Spanish government decided to build a proper capital city in *Nuevo Mexico,* with a traditional central plaza and a palace for the provincial governor. Franciscan missionaries soon followed, hoping to convert the natives to Christianity. Gradually over the years, oppressive taxes and forced labor led to the famous Pueblo Revolt of 1680. The Spaniards were defeated and left for a location near today's El Paso.

Not to be deterred, the Spanish reclaimed their important capital city in 1692. A long, uneasy peace among the Spanish, the newer settlers, and the Indians led up to the time in 1864 when the U.S. Army arrived to take over Santa Fe. New Mexico had been an American Territory since 1850. But it took a war with Mexico to effectively cut Santa Fe from formal ties with Mexico. And so, Santa Fe lived on as a fascinating polyglot of people and cultures.

The faces of Santa Fe speak volumes about the city's heritage. American Indian, Hispanic and Anglo artists, celebrities, and wide-eyed visitors mingle in the great plaza and down the narrow, winding side streets. The Palace of Governors faces the plaza, and on its covered portico, Indians from various tribes offer their traditional and contemporary crafts and jewelry for sale. Modern galleries and shops along the other sides of the plaza display fabulously expensive objets d'art by some of the nation's best-known artists.

Welcoming all these disparate entities is the Hotel St. Francis, just one block southwest of the historic plaza. The hotel was built in 1923, so the roaring twenties influence is evident, but the wrought-iron touches and clay tile floors suggest its southwestern setting. Refurbished antiques, light fixtures from the original state capitol and an old Chicago theater, and the hotel's 1930s switchboard are all somehow shown off in this eclectic ambiance. Formal afternoon tea is served in grand English style daily in the elegant lobby. Modern conveniences such as a personal safe and refrigerator in each guest room, and an honest-to-goodness concierge service in the lobby round out the cosmopolitan ambiance.

The St. Francis exterior, with its bright blue awnings and collonaded front, would be at home almost anywhere, but here it is, in a city known for its ubiquitous pueblo-style buildings, which even include grocery stores, parking garages, and dry cleaning establishments.

The original 1880s building, on the site of today's St. Francis, was The Palace Hotel. In 1915, it was renamed De Vargas Hotel, which in 1922 was destroyed by fire. The owners rebuilt the structure in 1923 by joining an 1888 two-story building to the new three-story building. One of the banquet facilities in the St. Francis is called the De Vargas Room—a reminder of the hotel's origins.

The fireplace was discovered behind a wall during restoration of the lobby.

A lovely surprise was revealed during its 1986 restoration. Sealed off in an earlier renovation was a beautiful, ornate fireplace, now the focal point of the lobby as it surely must have been onetime in the past.

In the late 1930s and 1940s, the state capitol building was just across the street, so the St. Francis was predictably a gathering place for elected state officials and their staffs. Who knows how many far-reaching decisions were actually arrived at in the unofficial precincts of the hotel's bar? A huge blackboard kept patrons up to date on such diverse items as election results and World Series scores.

Because there are visitors who mistakenly believe they have left the United States when they arrive in Santa Fe, the hotel's concierge must handle odd questions and requests. Do we need passports? Can we drink the water? Do the natives speak English? And to top it off, the U.S. Postal Service occasionally seems unaware that New Mexico became the 47th state in 1912. Often the mail goes to "old" Mexico before it is rerouted to Santa Fe. The concierge takes it all in stride and claims that, along with the city's fiestas, arts focus, architecture, and cuisine, the apparent mystery of the place simply adds to its lovability.

The St. Francis offers immediate entry into its historical setting. The St. Francis Cathedral, only blocks away, stands majestically at the end of San Francisco Street. It was begun by Archbishop Jean Baptiste Lamy in 1869. Lamy became well known as a real-life character in Willa Cather's *Death Comes for the Archbishop*.

The Loretto Chapel, on the Old Santa Fe Trail, contains a "miraculous" stairway with an intriguing story. The Sisters of Loretto prayed to St. Joseph for a stairway to the choir loft. Legend has it that an itinerant carpenter arrived and offered his assistance. He built a circular staircase with two complete turns, 33 steps, and no central support. When the nuns looked for the man to pay him, he was nowhere to be found and was never seen again. The sisters came to believe that St. Joseph himself had come and built the needed staircase. The lovely stairway still confounds architects and builders with its beauty and amazing construction.

Opposite: Detail of the cathedral doors.

Here in Santa Fe are Victorian surprises, a pink Scottish Rite Temple based on the Alhambra in Spain, cottages dating before the 1957 building code, and studios of renowned artists. The world-famous Santa Fe Opera Festival takes place just outside the city near the Jemez Mountain Range.

There is no effective cliché or easy, one-sentence description of Santa Fe, but the Hotel St. Francis sits comfortably in the heart of this unusual, to say the least, American Rocky Mountain city.

Opposite: The Cantina lounge at La Fonda.

HOTEL ST. FRANCIS

LA FONDA
Santa Fe, New Mexico

Perhaps the most recognizable landmark in Santa Fe is La Fonda, its massive, multi-level adobe style proclaiming its Hispanic genesis. A small *fonda* (inn) was already in place when Santa Fe was founded in 1610 by Spanish conquistadors, who had been in the area since the 1550s. The city, and indeed all of what is now New Mexico, remained a part of Mexico until the mid-1800s. In 1846, General Stephen W. Kearny and his U.S. Army troops rode in and proclaimed it a territory of the U.S. Just as had happened shortly before at Las Vegas, the city's inhabitants offered no resistance.

The old Spanish capital had already been well established as the western terminus of the Santa Fe Trail as far back as 1821. The Missouri to Santa Fe route was the main path for commercial travelers, westbound settlers and miners, the U.S. Army, and a host of outlaws and highwaymen, until the railroad arrived in the late 1870s. The little adobe inn was right at the end of the trail at Santa Fe's plaza.

Following Kearny's "conquest," a celebratory ball took place at La Fonda, attended by soldiers, citizens, and a notorious gambling lady, Doña Tules Barcelo. The story goes that Doña Barcelo had bribed her way to the posh affair by offering Kearny a loan to pay for the ball.

The hotel went through two name changes and a complete rebuilding before once again becoming La Fonda as it looks today. Known as the U.S. Hotel and later The Exchange Hotel, 70 years of its history were spent in rough-and-tumble days and nights of gambling, drinking, and that odd form of justice known as "the code of the West." Hangings and shootings were not uncommon on the premises.

During the Civil War, Confederate General H. H. Sibley and some of his staff reached the hotel. It was there that the general heard of the Confederate defeat in nearby Glorieta Pass. That battle marked the last time Southern troops attempted to cross New Mexico borders.

John Martin bought The Exchange and for a time managed to upgrade both its reputation and its cuisine. Mrs. A. B. Davis leased the hotel next, but when she left, a real decline set in. Soon it was nothing more than a common boardinghouse. In 1913, the interior was the victim of a devastating fire. Finally, the old adobe building was razed by World War I tanks during a rally for Victory Bond sales.

Nineteen twenty-two saw the rebirth of La Fonda. Public investments paid for its reconstruction on the original site. Shortly after its reopening, the Atchison Topeka & Santa Fe Railroad bought the property and promptly leased it to Fred Harvey. Harvey hired architect John Gaw Meem to redesign the interior, and designer Mary Colter to refurnish it. The ambiance they achieved remains to this day.

The famous "Harvey Girl" waitresses held forth for 40 years. During World War II, many of La Fonda's guests were atom bomb scientists on their travels to and from nearby Los Alamos. Neils Bohr, Edward Teller, and Enrico Fermi were among them.

In 1968, the property was acquired by the current owners, the Corporacion de La Fonda. Beginning in the 1970s, Santa Fe was already becoming a tourist mecca, and by the 1980s it was definitely the "place to be." In 1985, during excavations for a carriage house, Spanish artifacts that predated the Pueblo Revolt of 1680 were discovered. The rare, valuable artifacts were sent to the Museum of New Mexico for safekeeping.

St. Francis Cathedral as seen from the balcony of a guest room.

Modern hostelry that it is, with its up-to-date conveniences, La Fonda, like its home city, is an array of indigenous wonders. Traditional Mexican tin works,

ornate wood carvings, decorative paintings, arched entryways, *bancos* (built-in benches), and *nichos* (niches for artworks) make this hotel unmistakably a product of historic influences. The huge lobby is like a community within the larger community.

We tend to forget how much older the Spanish/Mexican involvement in our country is than that of the Northern European/Pilgrim. Santa Fe is a good reminder, a living-history museum in itself. It is the oldest state capital in the country, and *El Palacio Real* (The Royal Palace) is one of only two in the 50 states. The other is in Hawaii. The adobe Palacio Real is the oldest U.S. government building and was home to the first New Mexico Territory governor, Lew Wallace, author of *Ben Hur*.

It would be presumptuous to try to describe all the fascinating discoveries awaiting visitors to La Fonda. Perhaps it's just as well. To explore this hotel and its setting on one's own is an important aspect of the cultural experience of Santa Fe.

Opposite: Today's entrance to La Posada.

LA POSADA DE ALBUQUERQUE
Albuquerque, New Mexico

The original spelling of Albuquerque had an additional "r". It was named for a Spanish viceroy, the Duke of Alburquerque, in 1706. It is strongly believed that the city had its dim beginnings when conquistador Coronado and his entourage spent the winter of 1540 along the Rio Grande, just a few miles north of present-day Albuquerque. Spaniards drifted in, in ever-increasing numbers, and eventually the site was known as *Bosque Grande de San Francisco Xavier, bosque* designating it as a thickly wooded area. By the time the New Mexico Territory was declared a part of the U.S., the extra "r" in the city's name had been dropped. It was really superfluous in the pronunciation anyway.

Despite its very definite Spanish origins, Albuquerque became an Anglo enclave following the arrival of the Atchison Topeka & Santa Fe Railroad in 1885, and six years later it officially became an incorporated city. New Mexico was made the 47th state in 1912. In 1937, the famous Chicago to Los Angeles Route 66 opened. Part of the historic highway was along Central Avenue in the heart of Albuquerque.

Hotelier Conrad Hilton enters the story in 1939. Born in San Antonio, New Mexico, Hilton had a dream of building a great hotel in his native state. Albuquerque was booming. The railroad and Route 66 made it an important transportation hub.

The first Albuquerque Hilton with its 60-foot sign was the state's tallest structure. It was a showcase for the talents of New Mexico architects, artists, and craftspeople, and a veritable jewel of Southwestern culture with balconies, large arched lobby, hand carved furniture, murals, and American Indian touches. By the 1960s, a larger Hilton was built a few miles away and the old hotel's name was changed to The Plaza. A few additions were made but an inevitable decline set in. In the early 1980s, the sad metamorphosis resulted in its becoming not much more than a "flophouse," ignored by the visitors of that era.

Then in 1984, an exciting plan allowed new owners to invest millions in the once grand hotel. The city helped with a grant, and there was enthusiastic support from the National Register of Historic Places. Carefully and methodically, old photos were gathered, local craftspeople were hired, and the old Hilton took shape once more.

The award-winning result was now named La Posada de Albuquerque. And so it remains in its regained success, an echo of the past when Conrad Hilton chose to announce his engagement to Zsa Zsa Gabor there in 1942.

When the Southwestern Resorts Associates bought the old Hilton in 1983, they went to a lot of trouble to trace down original furnishings and fixtures that had been torn out by the former owner. What the Associates couldn't locate, they reproduced at great expense. Fortunately, the ever-growing interest in preserving worthwhile historic properties makes La Posada de Albuquerque a mecca for guests seeking not just an overnight stay, but an experience of historical connection to be tucked away as a precious memory.

There are 114 guest rooms, all furnished differently, and outfitted with the comforts of modern installations. During the 1984 renovation, a beautiful

Local artisans contributed to the hotel's charm.

fountain from Juarez, Mexico, was added to the lobby. Hotel staffers fuss each day over its enormous arrangement of fresh flowers. The lobby's floor tiles are original and so is a portion of its woodwork, as well as the key rack behind the registration desk. The view into the atrium from the mezzanine level is a treat to be enjoyed at every opportunity.

Albuquerque's setting includes evidence of native inhabitants dating back at least 10,000 years and perhaps much further. Later, Anasazi Indians (the "ancient ones") lived in their communities strung out across northern New Mexico from 1100 to about 1300 c.e. On the edge of the city some 17,000 petroglyphs testify to the old, highly developed cultures.

Today their descendants live and celebrate with pow-wows and feast days in 19 separate pueblos, reservations visited by over 300,000 aficionados of the great American native Southwest heritage. Rules of etiquette and respect are necessary when visiting these sovereign nations. Although their current land areas are mere portions of the original homelands, the pueblo governments are in charge. Special sacred sites are not open to the public as is the case with many private religious rituals. Photographing and sketching are usually forbidden, although for a small fee sometimes allowed. If one keeps in mind that these sites are not tourist attractions but rather the homes of private families, it is understandable that courtesy is all-important.

Named from the word *sandia* for watermelon, because of the color that tints the mountains at sunset, Albuquerque's Sandia Mountains offer skiing, fossil hunting, wildlife watching, and a spectacular tram ride to Sandia Peak at well over 10,000 feet. For those more interested in riparian discoveries, there are the cottonwood-lined banks of the Rio Grande to explore. Five very visible extinct volcanoes stand in the Petroglyph National Monument to the west of the river so celebrated in the history of the American West. And maybe on one of these nature tours, a roadrunner, New Mexico's state bird, will dash along on the side of the road.

Old Town, a historic district, is just off the city's center where the old Hispanic heart of the city still beats. San Felipe de Neri Church is one of its treasured landmarks. Some 150 famous galleries and shops wait to be discovered, many in old adobe buildings. The works of native potters, jewelry-makers, metal artisans, and designers of distinctive Indian fetishes and kachinas (Hopi dancing figures) abound in Old Town shops. The 350-year-old plaza is a welcome respite from which to drink in all the historical nuances of this unusual seat of an ancient North American legacy.

La Posada had its beginnings as a Hilton Hotel. (Courtesy: La Posada de Albuquerque, New Mexico)

Opposite: The gazebo just outside the Lodge at Cloudcroft.

THE LODGE AT CLOUDCROFT
Cloudcroft, New Mexico

At two o'clock on a Sunday morning in June 1909, a fire broke out in the roof. Within an hour and a half, the lodge was burned to the ground. One of the kitchen boilers had exploded, sending parts high into the air over the town of Cloudcroft. Everyone in the vicinity— staff, guests, and neighbors—pitched in to save what they could.

Miraculously, no one was seriously injured. The manager was able to secure rooms in nearby cottages and to arrange for meals to be served in the Pavilion. Not be daunted, most of the guests remained in town for the duration of their planned vacations. But that was the end of the 1901 lodge built and operated by the Alamagordo and Sacramento Mountain Railway that delivered passengers right to the door at 9,000 feet above sea level.

Within two years, The Lodge was rebuilt on a higher and better-suited site and quickly became a favorite retreat in summer, with its naturally air-conditioned mountain atmosphere. By the time the Territory of New Mexico became a state in 1912, the new Lodge was well established as a destination resort. Renovations by a succession of owners have not altered its general appearance, nor its tradition of hospitality and excellent cuisine, including southwestern specialties.

The Lodge has high-ceilinged guest rooms and suites furnished in turn-of-the-century decor, but with all modern conveniences, it boasts a nine-hole mountain golf course, one of the highest and oldest in the country. In winter, when the average snowfall is 105 inches, the golf course becomes cross-country ski terrain. In any season, the view from the copper-domed Tower Room includes the distant gypsum wonderland of White Sands National Monument, and sunsets never forgotten. Incidentally, the Tower is a favorite spot for wedding ceremonies.

Some interesting historical tidbits involve The Lodge. Conrad Hilton was manager there in the 1930s. Hilton was a New Mexico native, and left his mark on several of the state's hostelries before broadening his scope to international proportions. Movie stars Clark Gable, Gilbert Roland, and Judy Garland were among the famous personalities who stayed there as guests. And so did Pancho Villa!

The Lodge has its own very special ghost. She is a young, red-haired beauty, whose lover "found her in the arms of another," after which she disappeared never to return, except as a lovely apparition sometimes wandering in the halls. Her name is Rebecca, and the Lodge's restaurant and lounge are named for her.

Burro Avenue is the main street of Cloudcroft, a town with no traffic lights. In its rarefied high-altitude air, visitors learn to walk slowly to keep from gasping while watching the locals bustle about at a normal pace. A few miles below Cloudcroft, High Rolls

High in the Tower is a tiny sitting room.

and Mountain Park farms produce their famous cherries, inspirations for an annual festival, long a tradition on the western slopes of the Sacramento Mountains.

To the north from The Lodge is the Mescalero Apache Reservation. Within an easy day's drive are Ruidoso (a horse racing center), Capitan (home of Smokey Bear), the International Space Hall of Fame, Apache Point Observatory, and the Valley of Fires lava fields.

The Lodge at Cloudcroft is the perfect getaway place in any season. The Mexican border at El Paso/Ciudad Juarez, just over 100 miles away, is a favorite destination for shopping, museums, and Chamizal

The spa just outside the lodge.

Memorial Park. The world's largest gypsum dunes, known as White Sands National Monument, are only 35 miles from The Lodge.

Even if you don't like strenuous activities—and most seem strenuous at this altitude—what could be more alluring than sitting in front of The Lodge's big, copper-hooded fireplace, sunk down in a comfy leather couch with a good book or a circle of friends?

Opposite: Central plaza, Las Vegas, New Mexico: in 1877 the windmill served as a gallows. (Courtesy: Citizen's Committee for Historic Preservation)

THE LODGE AT CLOUDCROFT

Las Vegas ("the meadows"), New Mexico, was founded in 1835 when the area was a part of the Republic of Mexico. A formal ceremony recognized the Mexican land grant to the 29 Mexican citizens who chose the townsite. The surrounding 500,000 acres were to serve as common land for grazing and farming. The settlers built a typical southwest village, complete with a central plaza, one-story adobe houses, and an adobe church, Our Lady of the Sorrows of Las Vegas. American soldiers of the 1840s, coming upon Hispanic towns like Las Vegas, thought they were seeing a huge system of kilns. The flat-topped adobe buildings seemed unlikely houses. The little settlement in Mexico's northeastern reaches sat just south of the Santa Fe Trail where it crossed the Gallinas River. The town soon served as a market place for wagon trains that had to be restocked as they headed through the plains and the Sangre de Cristo Mountain Range on their way to Santa Fe at the end of the trail.

In 1846, the United States Army of the West, under the command of General Stephen W. Kearny, neared Las Vegas. On August 15, General Kearny rode on horseback into the town plaza where the men of the town had gathered. Kearny climbed to the roof of an adobe building and declared the area a territory of the United States and himself as governor! Considering his action a fait accompli, he then headed for Santa Fe and further conquering.

The turmoil of the Mexican War and the revolt of the New Mexican Pueblo Indians ensued. When the Taos Pueblo revolt of 1847 was finally crushed, Las Vegas resumed its role of trading and commerce on the Santa Fe Trail. The route now also served U.S. troops whose wagon trains, as well as those of civilians and mail carriers, were relentlessly attacked by Apache and Ute Indians. By the 1850s, English-speaking Anglos had arrived to take advantage of the strategic site close to the protection of the new Fort Union, nearby to the north. But peace still did not reign. Confederate and Union troops battled in the area during the Civil War, and yet traffic on the Santa Fe Trail grew steadily.

Meanwhile the town grew in reputation for its outlaws, lawmen, murders and lynchings. There were some 50 years of uncommon violence—even for the so-called "wild west." For four years a "hanging windmill" stood in the plaza where both legal hangings and lynchings were held as public events. Stagecoach and train robberies plagued travelers, and perpetrators met their destiny in the plaza on the windmill. Billy the Kid, Jesse James, Doc Holliday, Wyatt and James Earp, and the leader of the notorious Dodge City Gang, known

by the name of "Hoodoo Brown," frequented Las Vegas. Through it all, Las Vegas managed to survive as a commercial center.

The lobby makes a comfortable, cheery area where locals and guests gather.

With the arrival of the Atchison, Topeka and Santa Fe Railroad in 1879, it was clear that a hotel was needed. After all, Las Vegas was now the first railroad port-of-entry in New Mexico. Pioneers Romero and Jean Pendaries built The Plaza, the "Belle of the Southwest," for $25,000 in 1882. The "Belle," however, immediately fell on hard times, and inept management forced its closing in 1886. Renovation and new managers allowed The Plaza to reopen the same year, and up until 1900 it served as a meeting and stopover place for organizations and associations of the Southwest. Doc Holliday and his companion, Big Nose Kate, as well as the notorious Vincente Silva, and a variety of Billy the Kids (perhaps occasionally the real one) frequented the hotel. A railroad strike and a depression resulted in more bad times for The Plaza until 1913, when silent film star Romaine Fielding made it his headquarters and film studio. For five months the hotel was renamed Hotel Romaine. That old name, although faded, can still be seen on the west facade.

Next Tom Mix, of cowboy film fame, took over and the hotel's name became The Plaza once more. Mix's movie company used the nearby western landscapes and sometimes the hotel itself in his popular motion pictures. Then once again The Plaza fell into disrepair. It wasn't until the late 1960s when a local entrepreneur, Lucy Lopez, brought it back to life. Through the 1970s, the hotel and coffee shop flourished.

Its final and most meaningful comeback was accomplished in 1982 when careful research and historical investigation by the Plaza Partnership, Ltd., now its current owners, resulted in complete restoration and yet another reopening. The hotel was soon added to the National Register of Historic Places.

Italianate in exterior style, The Plaza is a comfortable, historic center for those who come either on business or to explore the once rowdy town and its surrounding southwest charm. The friendly Plaza lobby has a beautifully restored white tin ceiling and two walnut staircases that lead to the second and third floors. The cheerful, informal dining room looks out to the old town plaza. A lounge/bar often features live entertainment. A variety of local walking tours begin at the hotel. Upstairs are single rooms (one is octagonal) and suites. Wide corridors give a feeling of old-fashioned hospitality. Rooms reflect the original architectural styles and decor of the historic hotel. Lucky guests will get a room facing the plaza, site of infamous goings-on that took place once upon a time.

One of the charming aspects of a stay at The Plaza is the wide variety of live entertainment, either in the lounge or the lobby. An American Indian artist/musician named George Deer Tracks Tyler may play haunting music on one of his beautifully crafted flutes. Or Antonia Apodaca, a traveling performer for the Smithsonian Institution, could regale her audience with songs and accordion music once played by her Hispanic ancestors.

Las Vegas holds many surprises. While one expects and finds old adobes, the town's stone buildings are unexpected. The arrival of the railroad enabled the importation of stone masons along with their building materials. By 1879, the town was dominated by wealthy merchants whose choices for architecture included Queen Anne, Romanesque, Eastlake, Italianate, Classical, and Gothic Revival. Today, Las Vegas has more than 900 buildings on the National Register of Historic Places.

In the late 1860s, *Nuestra Senora de Dolores* Catholic Church was built of randomly fit sandstone blocks, cut from a local quarry. When finished, it was the largest stone building in New Mexico.

Throughout the area, irrigation ditches called *acequias* wander through the town and surrounding farmlands. Each spring, neighbors join in clearing away brush and debris to keep the precious water flowing freely. Sluices insure that water can be delivered where and when it is needed.

New Mexico's long history—from the Pueblo Indian civilizations to Spanish exploration, to its role on the American western frontier, and to statehood—can be easily explored from its historic hotels. And the town of Las Vegas is an excellent microcosm of the state's flamboyant past. On the town bridge over the Gallinas River is a plaque announcing that Spanish Conquistador Coronado crossed there in 1541. To the north of town is Wagon Mound, the famous landmark that assured wagon trains they were on the Santa Fe Trail.

Today's Las Vegas capitalizes on its authentic western and southwestern heritage with fiestas, llama treks in the mountains, and the annual Rails 'n Trails Days celebration in June. From its place on the old plaza, the hotel remains the heart of this multi-cultural, multi-lingual, hospitable community.

*Opposite: Entrance to
Taos Inn.*

THE HISTORIC TAOS INN
Taos, New Mexico

For almost a thousand years, the Taos people have lived near their sacred mountain and hidden Blue Lake; four hundred years ago, Spanish conquistadors came exploring; a hundred years later Hispanic missionaries and settlers arrived, followed by Mexicans, and last to come were European and American artists and seekers of a simpler life. The resulting uncommon richness of this layered culture is the setting for The Historic Taos Inn in the village of Taos.

A conglomeration of nineteenth-century buildings that once ringed a small plaza with a central well makes up the current inn. The well is now a fountain in the plaza-turned-lobby. Four massive vertical *vigas*—timbers from mountain forests—reach two-and-a-half stories into a skylighted cupola. The inn retains the thick adobe walls, arches, *nichos* (niches), and *bancos* (built-in adobe benches) of the classic Santa Fe style of architecture. Colorful Indian rugs and blankets hang over the second-floor balconies. Originally called the Hotel Martin, the establishment opened in 1936. One of its walls behind a wooden-stick "coyote" fence on the far side of the swimming pool dates back to the 1600s. But for its 1930s neon thunderbird sign, the inn could be mistaken for a private home.

It was in 1889 or 1890 that the flamboyant Dr. Thomas Martin arrived in Taos and bought a house just off the main town plaza. "Doc" Martin was the only physician in town for 30 years. He is said to have been "irascible but lovable," and often accepted chickens and vegetables in payment for his services. He cared for many of the Taos Pueblo Indians, and amassed a collection of Indian art. Martin began buying up the buildings around the little plaza, renting them to writers and artists. When Martin died in 1934, his widow, Helen, bought the remaining nearby buildings, and with the help of Doc's former patients opened the Hotel Martin two years after his death. Later owners changed the name to the Taos Inn.

The inn's restaurant, named for Doc Martin, is the actual site of his home. A small alcove once served as his delivery room and surgery. In those early days, passersby would look in and see who was a patient on any given day. The dining room draws discriminating food-lovers from around the country and, indeed, the world. For many years, the inn has been honored with awards for its outstanding wine list.

Each guest room is uniquely furnished with Spanish Colonial antiques and northern New Mexican handmade pieces. Several rooms have working adobe fireplaces. These charming fireplaces are hallmarks,

not only of the Taos Inn, but also of most of the original area buildings as well. Nationally recognized adobe artist Carmen Velarde has restored the fireplaces with a loving skill. She takes obvious joy in thrusting her hands into the mud and straw mixture, and smoothing it out with strong, turquoise-bedecked fingers. Velarde demonstrates what writer Mabel Dodge Luhan called the "sacredness" of using the very earth we walk on to shape into a home.

The fountain from a tiny plaza, now enclosed in the inn.

In the lobby are conversation areas where locals and visitors meet over southwest specialties of food and drink. The Taos Inn lobby is a kind of community living room where, on any given evening, you could be rubbing shoulders with a celebrity writer, artist, musician, actor, or just plain folk! A Pueblo Indian with neat, ribboned braids may be at the desk when you check in.

The Adobe Bar is known as the artist center of Taos. The entire lobby and bar area comprises a veritable gallery of southwest

Indian, Hispanic, and Anglo art works, an unmistakable sign of the town's creative, multicultural heritage.

It's not difficult to understand how sixteenth-century Spaniards thought they had discovered a legendary golden city when they came upon the natives' Taos Pueblo in 1540. Earth, straw, and water shaped into multi-level community dwellings and maintained through a millennium still confound today's amazed visitors. The adjoining lands of the Taos Pueblo make up a sovereign nation within the United States. Thick adobe walls and timber *vigas* of its surprisingly condo-like form are the prototypical features for most of the buildings in town.

The Taos Pueblo land originally comprised some 300,000 acres, including Taos Mountain and Blue Lake where ceremonials took place. Over the years, encroaching settlement by outsiders reduced the actual holdings to about 50,000 acres of tribal land. By 1906, the Forest Service established Carson National Forest which included the sacred watershed. Timber cutting and recreational activities were allowed. In a long, uphill fight to regain their land, the Taos people eventually took their case to Washington. Elders of the tribe sat praying softly in the visitor gallery during Senate deliberations, and when the vote was announced in their favor, the old *cacique* (medicine man) raised his walking stick in triumph. In 1970, President Nixon signed a bill into law, and the sacred lands became once more the sole domain of the native people. R. C. Gordon-McCutchan, author of *The Taos Indians and the Battle for Blue Lake,* likens the story to Roman Catholics winning back a lost Vatican or Anglicans repossessing Canterbury Cathedral.

Artists and writers who, in the 1920s, came to Taos searching for spiritual meaning following the chaos of the World War I began a tradition that is alive and well at the end of the century. The great brew of disparate cultures still bubbles heartily, and visitors to the area are free to make their own personal discoveries there. A stay at the Taos Inn provides easy access to the famous pastel views of New Mexico's landscapes, masterpieces of subtlety.

Whether one goes in winter to enjoy the powder slopes of Taos Ski Valley, in other seasons to explore historic and natural treasures, or to discover a real "Indian" summer, The Historic Taos Inn is a vessel that holds it all together. One has only to choose between friendly celebration in the dining room or lounge, and quiet wonder alone by an adobe fireplace. It's a hard choice.

SOUTH DAKOTA

The Alex Johnson Hotel, Rapid City
The Franklin Hotel, Deadwood

From its very beginnings, the Alex Johnson Hotel was dedicated to celebrating the culture of the Sioux Indians who had hunted, fished, camped, and raised corn throughout the Black Hills of today's South Dakota. The Teton Sioux, the quintessential plains Indians, had by 1750 become an equestrian, buffalo-dependent people.

The incorporation of their symbols and art went a long way toward the hotel becoming known as "The Showplace of the West."

In 1927, groundbreaking took place for the Chicago Northwestern Railroad's 11-story hotel. It was named for the man who, after an illustrious career in law, had chosen not only to live in the area but had immersed himself in the Sioux traditions. In 1933, Alex Johnson was made blood brother to the Sioux Chief, Iron Horse. Johnson's striking portrait in the role of Chief Red Star hangs in the lobby of the Alex Johnson.

The hotel's management is absorbed in the continual restoration of the building to its original glory. No small task that, for over the years many of its early Indian murals and designs were painted over in repair or renovation work.

In 1991, preoccupation with authenticity led Jodie Hertenstein, then general manager, and Cynthia Day, then marketing director, to seek advice from a Sioux medicine man in a ceremony held for that purpose. The two women sat in darkness for over two hours while the medicine man prayed for wisdom about how various Sioux tribes should be represented in the halls of the upper floors being readied for restoration. He then communicated his messages to the women who recalled with wonder the beauty, mystery, and spirituality of their experience.

Old photographs reveal that the lobby looks very much as it did when the grand opening took place. The large fireplace of native fieldstone shows off area ranch brands on its wooden mantel. Beautiful wood beams are anchored in plaster cast Indian heads two stories above the lobby floor. Between the beams are designs based on Sioux beadwork. An eye-catching chandelier is constructed of war lances surrounded by bands of Indian symbols, including the ancient swastika. The lobby's tile floor reflects the belief of the Lakota Sioux in four sacred powers, colors, and directions. The use of circles in the design indicates the oneness of the earth and all its living things.

The presidential suite once served as the summer White House for the Franklin D. Roosevelt family on a visit to the area. The entire tenth floor was taken over by his entourage. Presidents Coolidge, Eisenhower, Ford and Reagan have also stayed at the hotel.

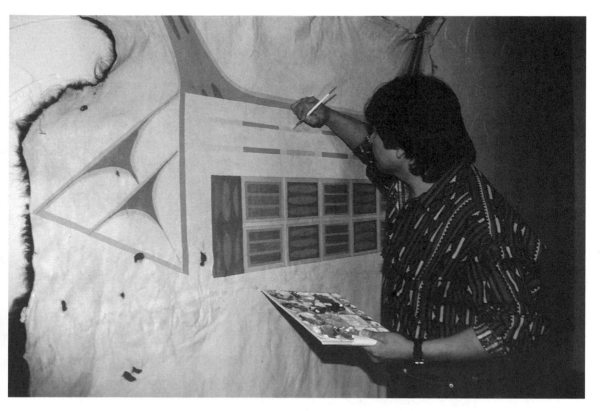

During World War II, Sunday dances took place in the ballroom, welcoming the military from a base nearby. Although it is now used for conferences and meetings, most of the ballroom's important features have been retained, including original murals of some of the region's natural grandeur. There are no less than five

Artist Norman Blue Arm adds a new piece of art to the lobby.

national parks within easy driving distance, not to mention the wide open beauty of the entire Black Hills country with its Rocky Mountain backdrop.

The hotel's exterior, with its surprising English Tudor-style facade, has changed hardly a bit since the 1920s. Brick and concrete construction is accented with Indian heads that look like giant, appliquéed nickels.

Just a short drive from Rapid City is Mount Rushmore, dedicated in July 1991, 50 years after its completion that was overshadowed by the beginning of World War II. Sculptor Gutzon Borglum helped select the granite outcropping site for his "patriotic statuary" project in the Black Hills. He began work on the head of Washington in 1927 and by 1939 the Lincoln, Jefferson and Roosevelt heads had been unveiled. It took nearly 14 years of drilling, chiseling, and blasting by 360 men, whose top pay was $1.25 per hour, to finish the gigantic, much-visited, monument.

Not far away is another mountain memorial in the making—this one a monument to Sioux Chief Crazy Horse, perhaps the best loved of all the great chiefs. Begun by sculptor Korczak Ziolkowski in 1948 as one man's dream and funded entirely by donations, the huge horse and rider will one day dominate the Black Hills landscape, ancestral home of Crazy Horse's people. Since the sculptor's death in 1982, the work has been carried on by the Ziolkowski family and associates who are utterly committed to the completion of the long-range project many of them may not live to see.

A great way to end an evening at the Alex Johnson is to watch the preparation of a house specialty called the "Landmark Coffee." Flaming rum in a cinnamon and sugar encrusted glass provides the base for the ceremonial addition of several other magical ingredients, each one swirled in with a flourish. The obligatory dollop of whipped cream completes the theatrics. It is a work of art. But to savor the concoction—now that's a whole new level of delight!

The Alex Johnson beckons to another time, another place in the history of the American west. The proximity of the Sioux reservations provides an opportunity to learn a balanced historical overview of the much-romanticized west. With just a little effort, one can imagine rumbling herds of buffalo and traveling bands of Sioux families. Ah, yes, they are gone now, but the spirit of their culture can still be enjoyed at this "Showplace of the West."

Alex Johnson's portrait as blood brother to the Sioux hangs over the lobby fireplace.

Opposite: The town trolley stops for passengers in front of the Franklin.

THE FRANKLIN HOTEL
Deadwood, South Dakota

During the rush to the Rockies for gold and other mineral treasure, communities came and went with the accompanying vagaries of mining enterprises. Many are now ghostly reminders of transient human habitation, whose almost obliterated streets are paths for wind-blown tumbleweeds. But some have found ways to survive, and their names evoke the somewhat preposterous romance of the west. Cripple Creek, Central City, and Deadwood—what lover of the frontier era doesn't associate notorious outlaws, nouveau riche prospectors, and cocky lawmen with those towns?

General George Armstrong Custer's highly publicized affection for the Black Hills in the Dakota Territory resulted in the rush to Deadwood. The tiny settlement was named for the burned and tornado-wounded forests that surrounded it. Some of Custer's men found placer gold deposits along area creeks in 1874, and Custer spread the word that even amateurs willing to spend time and labor could strike it rich there.

It didn't seem to matter that the Black Hills had been included in the Great Sioux Reservation by a treaty in 1868. Although the U.S. Army had been ordered to keep miners out, in 1875 President Grant withdrew the troops. Prospectors from failing mine operations in other parts of the country swarmed in, and Deadwood Gulch was one of their destinations. By 1876, the narrow, three-mile-long valley was the hub of panning and digging for gold—one of the last great gold rushes in the lower 48. Ditches, steam-run saw mills, hydraulic sluice boxes, flumes, dredges, and smelters soon followed, and for a few years the boom was on.

A fire in 1879, along with the waning of placer gold, spelled the beginning of the end of Deadwood's wildest days. According to Black Hills historian Watson Parker, ". . . mud and garbage combined with manure from horses, mules, and oxen to produce a remarkable slush and stench . . . ," and the creek that ran through the center of Deadwood was " . . . for a hundred years an open sewer. . . . " When lode mines in the nearby mountains were discovered, Deadwood managed to remain the business center of it all. The wealthy built their houses on the hillsides above the squalor. Many remain intact as reminders that, just as in other boom towns, a modicum of sophistication existed cheek by jowl with the struggling citizens below.

In the early days, there were 75 saloons in Deadwood. The first slot machines and the town's horse-drawn trolleys arrived in 1888. People died of lead poisoning (bullets), and many lives were snuffed out by "suspended sentences" (lynching).

Stagecoach travel was incredibly dangerous, one of the companies requiring people to change cash and gold dust to bank drafts before boarding a coach. First there were hostile Indians and then there were road agents, so hardly a trip was taken without loss of valuables or even lives.

Famous marshall and gunman Wild Bill Hickok left his new wife in Wyoming for the 1876 gold madness of Deadwood. He sat one day playing poker in the No. 10 Saloon with his back to the door. Jack McCall entered and shot him in the head, killing him. In Hickok's hand were the famous pair of black aces and eights—what would be called the dead man's hand. No one knows what the fifth card was.

Martha Canary (Calamity Jane) also arrived in 1876. Despite her reputation for being a boozy, loose-living, tough woman (she had come to the Black Hills disguised as a soldier), she is also remembered for her

The town of Deadwood in 1876. (Courtesy: The Franklin Hotel)

THE FRANKLIN HOTEL

care of victims of a smallpox epidemic. Poker Alice Tubbs, said to have been an Englishwoman, was a frequent visitor to Deadwood. Her businesses included banking and gambling, but her cigar-smoking presence at poker games made her one of Deadwood's most cherished characters. She lived until 1930. Through floods and fires, the doughty little town supplied those hallmarks of frontier history—gambling, drinking, and prostitution.

The investments and profits of Harris Franklin, a liquor dealer and cattle rancher, contributed the lion's share of capital for the Franklin Hotel, built in 1903. Franklin, who changed his name from Finklestein, was one of a small group of Jewish businessmen who settled in Deadwood. The Harris Franklin home on Van Buren Street, predictably high on a hill, is now a bed and breakfast establishment.

While the hotel was under construction, it became customary to allow passersby to add a brick to the monumental structure, many of them climbing high on the scaffolding to choose an imposing spot. A natural spring underneath the building was left in the basement to feed a fountain in the lobby above. The fountain has long since disappeared. The Franklin, a four-story brick and stone edifice, had 80 rooms (many with baths), steam heat, and two ladies' parlors. A grand ball celebrated its opening. Later an addition was built, but soon the Great Depression kept the town and hotel from prospering.

As late as 1981, Watson Parker wrote:

> *Deadwood prostitution continues to the present: There is no city ordinance against, nor is there much civic opposition to it. Pillars of the church and government often own the buildings housing the remaining "upstairs rooms," and the girls, at least, pay their rent with punctuality. Four houses still flourish, with perhaps twenty to thirty girls, and the police interfere only in case of a disturbance.*

Legalized gambling in 1989 saved Deadwood, as well as other old frontier towns along with their historic hotels, from slow death by neglect. Today the Franklin's beautifully tiled lobby floor is all but

obscured by banks of slot machines. But according to owner Bill Walsh, there were slots in the old days, too. In fact, most of today's gambling halls were originally saloons and they line the main street of Deadwood as they did a hundred years ago. The sounds, except for absent gunshots, are probably not much different—the

The lobby, now a gambling hall, still retains its original tiled floor.

ringing and clanging of slot machines, and the voices of hawkers luring visitors to "live" poker games. One plaintive singsong, "B. B. Cody's," that carries the length of the street can be heard from street-facing rooms upstairs in the Franklin.

From Deadwood's National Historic Places, the Black Hills and the Badlands stretch out, famous anew from some scenes in the movie *Dances with Wolves*. Within a day's journey are such wonders as Devil's Tower, Mount Rushmore, Chief Crazy Horse Monument, Indian Pow-wows, Custer State Park, and the Black Hills Passion Play.

Today's Franklin Hotel has been carefully restored and the rooms, now fully equipped with all modern conveniences, are furnished with antiques gathered from western towns and cities. Scores of rooms are named for the people who once stayed in them. The Kennedy and Teddy Roosevelt suites are elegant and spacious. Others celebrate their namesakes—Babe Ruth, Cecil B. De Mille, Buffalo Bill Cody, Lawrence Welk and John Wayne—with clever reminders of the famous guests.

Visitors come to Deadwood in summer to savor a real remnant of the old West, and many are attracted by the deep snows of Deadwood's winter, a virtual paradise for skiing and snowmobiling. Today's visitors to the Franklin are living out Deadwood's old tradition of year-round limited-stakes gambling in the incomparable beauty of South Dakota's Black Hills.

WYOMING

Brooks Lake Lodge, Dubois
The Irma, Cody

The year was 1922. Growing curiosity and appreciation for the American West meant thousands of travelers were looking for the most comfortable way to get there and then stay for a vacation. The south entrance to Yellowstone, the nation's first national park, was now open. The Chicago and Northwestern Railway had just completed the Teton

Mountain Route to the great park. Leaving Chicago at midnight, passengers arrived at Omaha at 3:15 p.m. the same day. The following evening at 7:15, the train pulled into Lander, Wyoming—the end of the tracks.

From there the Lander-Yellowstone Park Transportation Company took over. For $128 per person, the big high-powered buses, made by the White Truck Company, took travelers from Lander to Moran near the south entrance. The fare included meals and lodging. The buses passed through the Wind River Reservation where, according to the Lander evening newspaper of June 1922, passengers were "impressed and delighted with the picturesque life of Shoshone and Arapahoe Indian tribes who are being educated in domestic lines of endeavor after the ways of their white brothers." Bus drivers had to be "exceptionally good men" and earned $175 per month.

One of the favorite stopover places was the Brooks Lake Hotel, built that same year as an overnight lodging for the new route to Yellowstone. It was no easy task then to build and furnish a lodge in the Wyoming Rockies. Years later one of the truck drivers recalled, "We kept getting stuck in the trucks and had to unload fifteen of those old cast iron bath tubs. Six times."

Within two miles of the Continental Divide in the Shoshone National Forest, at an altitude of 9,300 feet, the log lodge offered "flatlanders" an excellent introduction to the Old West as they made their way to Yellowstone.

In less than two years, the lodge and ranch were bought by James T. Gratiot, who had a penchant for flashy dress including diamonds. Not surprisingly, he was known as "Diamond Jim" and the property became the Diamond G Ranch. It operated successfully as a camp and headquarters for extraordinary pack trips following such routes as the historic John Colter trails of 1807. For about $800 per person, a seven- or eight-day combination of horseback and rafting recreated the frontier experiences usually reserved for presidential parties and European royalty.

In an old Diamond G Ranch promotional piece, the following story of legendary mountain man Jim Bridger's adventure at the Continental Divide is told:

Old Jim Bridger, the scout who scorned soldiers and their aid and traveled so far that his lone journeys became mythology, fared little better in Jackson Hole. He found another route from the north into Yellowstone and the Hole and discovered Two-Ocean Pass. But his story of seeing a mountain climbing fish swim up one creek that flowed toward the Pacific and swim through a place this stream connected with another flowing toward the Atlantic, was promptly greeted with howls of mirth. But it was all true and later, confirmed as a fact, and Two-Ocean Pass, where Bridger saw the fish, is marked on government maps.

Brooks Lake was named for Wyoming's Governor Bryant B. Brooks (1905–1911) who wrote an article for the Wyoming State Journal in 1927. He described the lake he remembered from 1889 as, "quite clear, and I could see hundreds and thousands of mountain trout, great big fellows swimming about."

When the Depression hit businesses all over the country, the western dude ranches also felt the pinch and, inexorably, clientele dwindled. The Diamond G was not spared. For many years, the elegant lodge languished in disrepair and neglect. Several owners attempted to revive interest in dude ranching, but the cost of proper restoration and modernization was almost insurmountable. Sometime in the 1950s, the name was changed to Brooks Lake Lodge.

It wasn't until Dick and Barbara Carlsberg of California formed the Brooks Lake Trading Company in 1988 that a new life began in earnest for the historic ranch. The monumental restoration effort necessarily included new wiring, plumbing and masonry work for the six separate cabins and the main lodge. A wing with six guest rooms was added. Now the ranch lived up to its designation on the National Register of Historic Places.

The lodge's high-ceilinged Great Hall can easily convince guests they have entered an old European hunting lodge. Trophy heads and game animal skins hang on the walls. Groupings of wicker-furnished conversation areas suggest a leisurely pace.

Cabins and lodge rooms, each with its own theme, feature hand-crafted rustic lodgepole furniture. Lest all this suggests a "roughing it" atmosphere, it is readily apparent that comfort and western-style elegance are the real hallmarks of a stay at Brooks Lake Lodge.

There is a tackle shop for those wishing to try a hand at landing one of those "great big fellows swimming about." Guests who wish to ride horseback on the spectacular mountain trails are assigned their very own horses for the length of their stay, giving horse and rider a chance to become acquainted, much the same experience the original dudes had.

Brooks Lake Lodge is within a hour's drive of some of North America's grandest scenery—Yellowstone, of course, with its unique natural wonders; Jackson Hole, Wyoming's famous mountain-ringed bowl; plentiful glimpses of wildlife; and then, the Grand Teton Range, sharp daggers attacking the cobalt blue skies (named the "great breasts" by early French trappers).

When to go there? Ah, that is the question. The snowmobiling is so ideal that snowmobile manufacturers like to film their commercials there. Wildflower lovers will think the ranch is heaven in spring. Hikers and sportspeople of every stripe have all-weather choices. Meals, fishing tackle, horseback riding, and boats are included in room rates. So it is possible to custom-make your own special getaway among the lakes, streams, mountains, and meadows of historic Brooks Lake Lodge and Ranch.

The dining room.

In 1902, a beautiful young woman named Irma was engaged to be married. She was known as a fine horsewoman, and her father was understandably proud of her. His splendid new hotel, named for her, was just about finished, so he made its grand opening an engagement party for her. This was no ordinary event in the still wild "Equality State" of Wyoming. Irma was the only surviving daughter of Colonel William "Buffalo Bill" Cody—Pony Express rider, Army scout, originator and star of the world-famous "Wild West" show, and founder of the town of Cody.

Cody had immediately seen the need for a comfortable hostelry for travelers to the region. Plans for the hotel had called for a classic Italianate building, and when it opened it was luxurious and up-to-date, although somewhat scaled down from the architect's early conception. It quickly became the center of social life in Cody where ranchers, tourists, business people, and townspeople gathered. To understand why and how this historic hotel came to be, it is necessary to take a look at the life of the famous man who built it.

In 1867, William F. Cody was 21 and already had a reputation as a cavalryman and scout. He was hired by the Kansas Pacific Railroad to supply 12 buffalo a day as food for the men laying track. He shot from the saddle at a gallop with his 50-caliber, single-shot Springfield rifle he called "Lucretia Borgia." His spectacular riding and shooting earned the name "Buffalo Bill."

In 1883, Cody's first full-scale Wild West Exhibition opened in Omaha. For the next 30 years, audiences in the United States. and Europe saw live buffalo and elk, American Indians, bronc-busting cowboys, sharpshooters, stagecoaches, and pony express riders in extravaganzas of western adventure—always featuring an appearance by Buffalo Bill himself. Over 600 cast members and 500 animals rode the Wild West trains, crisscrossing the country and even sailing overseas to Europe.

Buffalo Bill died in Denver in 1917 and was buried nearby on Lookout Mountain, far from his Wyoming home. It is said his grave was heavily encased in concrete so his body could not be moved, even though the year before his death he had led a party to the top of Cedar Mountain in Cody to choose his burial place. Today on Cedar Mountain, the sculpture of a lone bison marks the spot. From this vantage point there is a grand view of the Big Horn Basin and Shoshone River Valley he loved so well.

The Irma Hotel is a fitting tribute to the Cody legacy. The huge barroom now serves as the main dining room where guests, townspeople, cowboys, and well-heeled business people still gather. Hearty, reasonably-priced meals cater to tourists as well as the ever-present working cowhands with their man-sized appetites. As a matter of fact, as a guest it's easy to get the feeling you're an "extra" on a western movie set.

By far the best-known feature of the Irma is its magnificent cherrywood bar. Some say it was a gift from Queen Victoria to Buffalo Bill and some say Cody commissioned it himself in France. In any case, it was shipped to New York from France, transported by train to Red Lodge, Montana, and the rest of the way to Cody by wagon.

Buffalo Bill Cody in the Irma's bar. (Courtesy: The Irma Hotel)

There are numerous reminders of the Irma's odd combination of Victorian and Wild West past. A bronze of Diana the Huntress stands atop the newel post of a stairway leading to the second-floor rooms, each one named for a character in the Irma's past.

Wild parties were not unusual in the old days. One of them in the 1920s resulted in bullet holes in the ballroom's tin ceiling, a tempting target for exuberant, gun-toting cowboys. Much of the original ceiling has been replaced, but the bullet holes are still there for all to see.

Until recently the late Bill Cody, a dead ringer for his famous grandfather, often visited the Irma. He ran a ranch for visitors, and took great pride and pleasure in sharing his memories of the old days when traffic, mostly horse but some "chugalong cars," streamed along the dirt streets towards Yellowstone Park.

One of the most ambitious and authentic attempts to portray the American West of the 1800s and early 1900s is Trail Town, the brainchild of Bob and Terry Edgar. They have brought 26 historic buildings to the site in Cody where Buffalo Bill and his partners surveyed for the town in 1885. The old wagon trail can still be made out between the rows of cabins, each with its own story of larger-than-life characters, including Butch Cassidy, buffalo-hunter Jim White, and Indian scout "Curly" who is said to have been involved in the battle of Little Big Horn. Jeremiah "Liver-Eating" Johnston is buried there with other notorious mountain men. Trail Town has a feeling of reality; no blinking neon signs or come-ons announce the presence of this remnant of American history. You have to care about the subject and then you'll find it—a step back in time lovingly reconstructed by the Edgars, who continue to save a precious heritage.

The Shoshone River, Heart Mountain, the rolling grasslands, and the Big Horn Mountains to the east are all here today as they were in the 1800s when white explorers and settlers came. What are no longer here are the bison and the roaming bands of American Indians for whom much of the area was sacred. Fortunately for posterity, the City of Cody's excellent Buffalo Bill Historical Center features an entire museum dedicated to the Plains Indians, known as the "First People." The center houses three other museums, one devoted to Buffalo Bill.

Its Whitney Gallery contains one of the world's finest collections of western art. The center's newest addition is the Winchester Arms Museum. Just outside the center, William F. Cody is memorialized as "The Scout" in a heroic sculpture by Gertrude Vanderbilt Whitney.

Cody as "Scout" at the Buffalo Bill Historical Center.

The Irma Hotel, constructed of native stone, still dominates downtown Cody and has not changed a whole lot since its frontier days. In fact, there is no better window on the old west than Buffalo Bill's own choice, the one he built for family, friends, and visitors that they might be comfortable on their visits to the heart of Wyoming's Cody Country.

APPENDIX

Alex Johnson Hotel
523 6th Street
Rapid City, SD 57701
120 guest rooms and suites
Member: AHH WEST
(605) 342-1210

The Broadmoor
Colorado Springs, CO 80906
700 guest rooms
National Register of Historic Places
(719) 634-7711

Brooks Lake Lodge
Dick and Barbara Carlsberg, owners
458 Brooks Lake Road
Dubois, WY 82513
6 lodge rooms and 6 cabins
Member: AHH WEST
(307) 455-2121

The Brown Palace Hotel
Rank Hotels North America
321 Seventeenth Street
Denver, CO 80202
230 guest rooms
Member: Preferred Hotels & Resorts Worldwide
Historic Hotels of America
(303) 297-3111

Castle Marne
1572 Race Street
Denver, CO 80206
9 guest rooms
National Register of Historic Places
Member: AHH WEST
(303) 331-0621

Cleveholm Manor
58 Redstone Boulevard
Redstone, CO 81623
16 guest rooms

Delaware Hotel
700 Harrison Avenue
Leadville, CO 80461
36 rooms and suites
Leadville National Historic District
Member: AHH WEST
(719) 486-1418

The Franklin Hotel
700 Main Street
Deadwood, SD 57732
75 guest rooms
Member: AHH WEST
(605) 578-2241

Gallatin Gateway Inn
Highway 191
Gallatin Gateway, MT
(406) 763-4672

Glacier Park Lodge
East Glacier, MT 59434
154 guest rooms
(406) 226-5551

The Historic Taos Inn
125 Paseo del Pueblo Norte
Taos, NM 87571
39 guest rooms
Member: AHH WEST
(505) 758-2233

Hotel Boulderado
2115 13th Street
Boulder, CO 80302
160 guest rooms (including an annex)
(303) 442-4344

Hotel St. Francis
210 Don Gaspar Avenue
Santa Fe, NM 87501
82 guest rooms
National Register of Historic Places
Member: AHH WEST, Historic Hotels of America
(505) 983-5700

The Irma
1192 Sheridan Avenue
Cody, WY 82414
40 guest rooms
Member: AHH WEST
(307) 587-4221

Izaak Walton Inn
U.S. Highway 2
Essex, MT 59916
31 rooms, 3 cabooses
Member: AHH WEST
(406) 888-5700

La Fonda
100 East San Francisco
Santa Fe, NM 87501
153 guest rooms
Member: Historic Hotels of America
(505) 982-5511

La Posada de Albuquerque
Second at Copper NW
Albuquerque, NM 87102
114 guest rooms
National Register of Historic Places
Member: AHH WEST
(505) 242-9090

The Lodge at Cloudcroft
1 Corona Place
Cloudcroft, NM 88317
58 guest rooms and suites
(505) 682-2566

The Peck House
Highway 40
Empire, CO 80438
11 guest rooms
National Register of Historic Places
Member: AHH WEST
(303) 569-9870

Plaza Hotel
230 Old Town Plaza
Las Vegas, NM 87701
38 guest rooms
National Register of Historic Places
Las Vegas Plaza Historic District
Member: AHH WEST
(505) 425-3591

The Pollard
2 North Broadway
Red Lodge, MT 59068
40 guest rooms and suites
Member: Historic Hotels of America
(406) 446-0002

The Prince of Wales Hotel
Waterton Lakes
Alberta, Canada TOK 2MO
90 guest rooms
(403) 236-3400

Redstone Inn
82 Redstone Boulevard
Redstone, CO 81623
35 guest rooms
National Register of Historic Places
Member: AHH WEST, Historic Hotels of America
(970) 963-2526

Sacajawea Inn
5 North Main Street
Three Forks, MT
33 guest rooms
National Register of Historic Places
(406) 285-6934

The Stanley Hotel
A Grand Heritage Hotel
333 Wonderview Avenue
Estes Park, CO 80517
92 guest rooms
Member: AHH WEST
(970) 586-3371

Strater Hotel
Main Avenue
Durango, CO 81302
93 guest rooms
Durango Historic District
Member: AHH WEST, Historic Hotels of America
(970) 247-4431

Inn at Zapata Ranch
Highway 150
Mosca, CO 81146
15 guest rooms
Member: AHH WEST
(719) 378-2356

SELECTED BIBLIOGRAPHY

Abbot, Carl, S. Leonard, D. McComb. *Colorado: A History of the Centennial State*. Niwot, Colorado: University Press of Colorado, 1982

Atkinson, Gail S. and Jim C. *Izaak Walton Inn*. Kalispell, Montana, 1985

Ayer, Eleanor. *Hispanic Colorado*. Frederick, Colorado: Jende-Hagan Book Corporation, 1982

Bancroft, Caroline. *Silver Queen*. 14th ed., Boulder, Colorado: Johnson Publishing Co., 1978

_____. *Tabor's Matchless Mine*. Boulder, Colorado: Johnson Publishing Co., 1960

Bertozzi-Villa, Elena. *Broadmoor Memories*. Colorado Springs, Colorado; The Broadmoor Publisher, 1993

Bidal, Lillian. *In Pursuit of a Railroad*. Cloudcroft, New Mexico, 1990

Blair, Kay Reynolds. *Ladies of the Lamplight*. Leadville, Colorado: Timberline Books, 1971

Boland, Mary. *The History of the Crystal Valley*. Glenwood Springs, Colorado: Redstone Corporation, (n.d.)

Breihan, Carl W. *Great Gunfighters of the West*. New York: First Signet Printing, 1977

Bryan, Howard. *Wildest of the Wild West*. Santa Fe, New Mexico: Clear Light, 1991

Burlingame, Merrill. *John M Bozeman: Montana Trailmaker*. Bozeman, Montana: Montana State University, 1983

Canning, Anne Smedley. *Early Estes Park*. Denver, Colorado, 1990

Clark, Ella, and Margot Edmonds. *Sacajawea of the Lewis and Clark Expedition*. Berkley, Los Angeles, London: University of California Press, 1979

DeWall, Rob. *Korczak, Storyteller in Stone*. Crazy Horse, South Dakota: Korczak's Heritage, Inc. (second revised printing), 1986

Djuff, Ray. *The Prince of Wales Hotel*. Waterton Park, Alberta: Waterton Natural History Association, 1991

Edwards, Aaron W. *My Cloudcroft*. Cloudcroft, New Mexico, 1982

Feinberg, John; T. Young; T. McFerrin; K. Slick; M. Stewart; S. Rychener. *Out and About in New Mexico*. Boulder, Colorado: AHHWEST, 1988

Foote, Alvin. *The Fabulous Valley*. Redstone, Colorado: Whitman-House (n.d.)

Gratiot, James T., and F. S. Scott. "The Diamond G. Ranch" ms. (n.d.)

Harrison, Louise C. *Empire and the Berthoud Pass*. Denver, Colorado: I. Martin Company, 1974

Herzog, Peter. *La Fonda, The Inn of Santa Fe*. The Press of the Territorian (n.d.)

Hetzler, Rosemary and John Hetzler. *Colorado Springs and Pikes Peak Country*. Revised Edition. Norfolk, Virginia: The Donning Co., 1989

L'Amour, Louis. *Reilly's Luck*. New York: Bantam, 1971

Luhan, Mabel Dodge. *Edge of the Taos Desert*. Albuquerque, New Mexico: University of New Mexico Press, 1988

Lynde, Francis. *Cripple Creek 1900*. Olympic Valley, Colorado: Outbooks, 1976

McCollumm, Oscar. *History of Marble, Colorado*. Marble, Colorado: 1983

McMillon, Bill. *The Old Hotels and Lodges of Our National Parks*. South Bend, Indiana: Icarus Press, 1983

McTighe, James. *Roadside History of Colorado*. Boulder, Colorado: Johnson Books, 1989

National Register of Historic Places, Department of the Interior

Nesbit, Paul. *Long's Peak*. Ninth Edition. Halstead, Kansas: Mills Publishing, 1990

Parker, Watson. *Deadwood: The Golden Years*. Lincoln, Nebraska: University of Nebraska Press, 1981

Pettem, Silvia. *Legend of a Landmark*. Boulder, Colorado: The Book Lode, 1986

Rinehart, Mary Roberts. *Through Glacier Park in 1915*. Boulder, Colorado: Roberts Rinehart, 1983

Sanford, Barbara Pollard. "The Pollard Hotel" (personal journal) Red Lodge, Montana (n.d.)

Smith, Duane A. *Rocky Mountain Boom Town*. Niwot, Colorado: University Press of Colorado, 1992

Ubbelohde, Carl. *A Colorado History*. Boulder, Colorado: Pruett Press, Inc., 1965

Zupan, Shirley. *History of Red Lodge*. Red Lodge, Montana, 1989

Other source materials include: brochures, maps, periodicals, newspapers, manuscripts and interviews.

INDEX